Jailbreak Out of History

The Re-Biography of Harriet Tubman

and

"The Evil of Female Loaferism"

by Butch Lee

KER
SPL
EBE
DEB
2015

Jailbreak Out of History: The Re-Biography of Harriet Tubman
Second Edition
ISBN: 978-1-894946-70-4

Kersplebedeb Publishing
CP 63560
CCCP Van Horne
Montreal, Quebec
Canada H3W 3H8

email: info@kersplebedeb.com
web: www.kersplebedeb.com
       www.leftwingbooks.net

Copies available from:
AK Press
674-A 23rd St.
Oakland, CA
94612

phone: (510) 208–1700
email: info@akpress.org
web: akpress.org

Please note that information about the sources of illustrations
in this book can be found on the publisher's website at
http://kersplebedeb.com/jailbreak-illustrations

Printed in the united states

CONTENTS

Jailbreak Out of History:
the Re-Biography of Harriet Tubman

Harriet Tubman (1823-1913)
nurse, spy and scout

JAILBREAK OUT OF HISTORY: HARRIET

Childhood & the Gathering Storm

FOCUS ON AMAZONS. About why we deal with real women as myths. Girls who never *really* existed. Yet and again, are all around us & that we can't bring ourselves to see. Cause seeing through white men's eyes is about non-vision of ourselves. So let's deal with a real Amazon.

Think about Harriet Tubman. Take six months. In fact, take a year & think. Break it on down. What does it mean to be the most famous New Afrikan woman in u.s. history? What does it mean to be stuck in that lie? What's the meaning of being famous while being hidden and dis-figured and dissed? Let's jailbreak Harriet Tubman out of white his-story and place her in Amazon and New Afrikan herstory. Her story, her people's story.

Harriet Tubman's life is a live weapon placed in our minds, showing us what it means to be an Amazon. Which is why the capitalist patriarchy has forbidden us to touch it for so long. **In this, maybe for the first time, we can see Amazons as a future force in the clash of peoples & nations.** Not as myths, but as players in the whole difficult course of world politics. We can also appreciate the bittersweet tang of reality, as the peeling away of layers of propaganda and disfigurement which have hidden Harriet from us exposes how much we assume and how little we've known.

New Afrikan women have already pointed out the significant pattern of Harriet's exclusion. Cultural critic bell hooks said recently: "I mean if we could recover Ida B. Wells and Harriet Tubman to the extent that we have recovered, say, Zora Neale Hurston, I think that's an important contrast because people want to bury that revolutionary black female history …"

Herstorian Deborah Gray White connects Harriet's treatment to a larger pattern in the mainstream history of slavery, in which Black women "were reduced to insignificance and largely ignored." In examining the influential historian Stanley Elkins, she points out:

> "That Elkins seemed to omit women altogether was accentuated by his description of slaves whom he identified as part of an American 'underground', those who never succumbed to Samboism. Among those mentioned were Gabriel, who led the revolt of 1820, Denmark Vessey, leading spirit of the 1822 plot at Charleston, and Nat Turner—an omission, conspicuous by its absence, was Harriet Tubman … If Elkins had really been thinking of slaves of both sexes he would hardly have forgotten this woman, who became widely known as the Moses of her people."

Patriarchal capitalisms, which only want Amazons to be exotic myths from forgotten ages, have hidden Harriet Tubman in her own fame. They both *trivialize* and *exceptionalize* her. These are tools of oppressor culture. The stripped-down and censored version of her life is told in elementary schools all over the u.s. empire. So much so that everyone thinks they know her story already, although they don't. Harriet Tubman was born in slavery in Maryland around 1820. She escaped to the North when she was 29, but kept returning secretly to the South again & again to help other slaves escape. For this she became known as "Moses." True statements. But by limiting her it becomes clever propaganda against her. And against her people.

Where patriarchy has been unable to deny that women do significant things, it denies the full meaning of what we do by trivializing them. Mary Daly, feminist philosopher, traces the enormity of what patriarchy has done to us. In ancient Greece the goddess Hecate (also known later as Artemis and Diana) was sometimes known as Trivia (and represented by a three-faced statue). That was also the name used for the inter-section of three paths, which in many old cultures were the sites of mystical power. She writes in *Gynecology*:

> "In light of the cosmic significance of the term *trivia* as the crossing of the three roads and of the goddess who bears this name, contemporary meaning of the term in English should be examined. The English term, which, according to Merriam-Webster, is derived from the Latin *trivium* (crossroads), is defined as 'common, ordinary, commonplace ... of little worth or importance: insignifi-cant, flimsy, minor, slight.' Of course, according to pa-triarchal values, that which is 'commonplace' is of little worth, for in a competitive hierarchical society scarcity is intrinsic to 'worth.' Thus gold is more important than fresh air, and consequently we are forced to live in a world in which gold is easier to find than pure air."

So to trivialize Harriet Tubman the capitalist patriarchy pic-tures her as an idealized woman by their definition, who makes a life of helping others. *Thus her deeds are squeezed into women's assigned maternal role as nurturer, helper, and rescuer of men (who then go on to do the important things).* But Harriet wasn't repping Mother Teresa. She wasn't even any kind of civilian at all. She was a combatant, a guerrilla, a warrior carrying pistol and rifle, fighting in her people's long war for freedom. A war that rocked the foundations of Amerikkkan society and that has never gone away.

Think about what it means to be called "Moses" (which was the code name other New Afrikans gave her, and which became Harriet's famous warrior name in the Anti-Slavery underground). When we check out the bible, we can see that Moses was a ruthless visionary, someone who forced the bold-est changes and risks upon his people so that they could sur-vive. Who led them out of captivity. To put it simply, Moses was a leader in a time of war. So, too, was Harriet Tubman.

What trivializing her as a "rescuer" also does is that it takes her out of her own politics. Harriet Tubman was a radical political figure, someone totally involved as a player in the great political ideas and military storms of her day. She was a guerrilla. Someone who lived and taught others to live by the communal and working-class New Afrikan culture that her people had planted in this difficult ground, and a Black Feminist to the end.

In her own lifetime, white people were referring to her as "superhuman," as "a woman who did what no man could do" (as if this were some exceptional standard). Thus, even then her white supporters needed to *exceptionalize* her, as something unique and singular. This made her less dangerous to them. Easier to handle. Less awesome. After all, picture a nation of Harriet Tubmans.

First of all, there was nothing mythical or superhuman about her. Harriet Tubman was one captive New Afrikan woman among many. And her most striking qualities were qualities she had in common with many other Afrikan women and children, who like her came out of a culture of communal resistance and strength. So to insist on her supposed unique individuality as a compliment, is actually denying her real identity.

Five generations on Smith's Plantation, Beaufort, South Carolina, 1862.

To Understand Harriet, We Must First Understand the War

If they think of it at all, people look back on the Underground Railroad in *civilian* terms, as a "movement" like Civil Rights. In fact, such comparisons are often made. But the Underground Railroad cannot be understood in civilian terms, *because New Afrikans then were not civilians.*

Here again, it's easy to let ourselves be fooled by the disinformation of patriarchal capitalist history. It's easy to not really understand the distinction between civilian and military.

The meaning of these distinctions is important to us, and yet we never think about it. Harriet wasn't an Amazon because she was oppressed, or even because she dissented or rebelled. You're only military if that's what you are. Just because you're oppressed doesn't mean you're at war. Just because you rebel or protest that doesn't make you a soldier. New Afrikans still are oppressed, but they certainly aren't at war in 2015. That may have been true in the 1960s, the mass ghetto uprisings and the role of the Black Panther Party and the Black Liberation Army, but it's not true of the Black Nation today.

When Harriet and the other jailbreak leaders were referred to back then as "conductors," when the chiefs of local Underground Railroad committees were always spoken of as "station masters" and "brakemen," that was cover. Civilian-sounding words for illegal military activity. Harriet and the rest of the Underground Railroad had military goals, had military strategy and tactics. It wasn't any accident that Harriet and many of the other guides were armed. They were armed as front-line guerrillas who moved through a genocidal terrain. They were soldiers on a military mission, even though they may have been wearing work clothes and not have had a patriarchal military hierarchy anywhere on them.

Remember, most euro-settler men back then in the South or on the frontier weren't civilians exactly, either, even though they, too, may not have worn what we recognize as uniforms.

Most white men there were armed, as a normal matter. Had to be, when you come to think of it. Most nations of the capitalist metropolis have histories of strict personal gun control, like England and Japan. There, the ruling class was afraid of class warfare. While in settler-colonialist societies such as South Afrika, the u.s.a., and Israel, settler men have always had armed and militarized mass cultures to help conquer and rule over the oppressed.

In its origins as a white men's invasion culture, Team USA itself may have looked civilian to us, but it was really military. The masses of armed settler men were their *own* military. Banding together in militias or Slave Patrols or Committees of Correspondence to commit genocide against Indians. And prison guard their Afrikan and women "property."

The ways of life, the culture created by the young Black Nation in this furnace, were centered on dangerous and illegal resistance of all kinds. Even their music and their personal lives were part of this resistance. *Because without such guerrilla activity they would have had no space or human life at all.* Those were the stakes. And the New Afrikan political struggle against this armed oppressor had definite characteristics; it was not only conspiratorial and communal, embracing all forms of resistance from illegal education and sly sabotage to violence, but its only goal was the *total destruction* of the enemy slave-owning society. That was understood by all. That is, that political culture was inescapably *military* in its full dimensions, just as its situation was military.

Being disarmed is not the same thing as being civilian. A distinction that patriarchal capitalism loves to mess over in our minds.

New Afrikan Women's Unique Situation

For captive women, as Deborah Gray White explains in *Ar'nt I a Woman? Female Slaves In The Plantation South*, their bondage had another dimension from men because of the threat of rape and the responsibilities for the children. Even escaping, which every prisoner naturally dreamt of, was something more difficult for most women, who almost always had children to care for.

William Still, Philadelphia "station master" of the Underground Railroad, said that because of the difficulties of fleeing with children "females undertook three times the risk of failure that males are liable to." Deborah Gray White says her own studies of plantation-prison runaways in different areas & times consistently show that women were a minority. "In North Carolina from 1850 to 1860, only 19 percent of the runaway ads described women. In 1850, 31.7 percent of the runaways advertised for in New Orleans newspapers were women."

Many of those women who did escape had to leave children behind. New Afrikan women also resisted violently, as White points out:

> "Some bondswomen were more direct in their resistance. Some murdered their masters, some were arsonists, and still others refused to be whipped. Overseers and masters learned which black women and men they could whip, and which would not be whipped. Sometimes they found out the hard way. Equipped with a whip and two healthy dogs, an Alabama overseer tied a woman named Crecie to a stump with intentions of beating her.

> "To his pain and embarrassment she jerked the stump out of the ground, grabbed the whip, and sent the overseer running. Women fought back despite severe consequences. An Arkansas overseer decided to make an example of

a slave woman named Lucy 'to show the slaves that he was impartial.' Lucy, however, was not to be made an example of. According to her son, 'she jumped on him and like to tore him up.' Word got around that Lucy would not be beaten. She was sold, but she was never again whipped."

Their greatest resistance was not in these individual acts of anger and bravery, but in what lay beneath it. New Afrikan imprisoned women created communal networks to sustain and guide each other.

"Slave women have often been characterized as self-reliant and self-sufficient," Deborah Gray White reminds us. "Yet, not every Black woman was a Sojourner Truth or a Harriet Tubman. Strength had to be cultivated. It came no more naturally to them than to anyone, slave or free, male or female, black or white. If they functioned in groups..."

Women more than men were the long-time core of a plantation's multi-generational population. The networks or women's sub-culture they created with their own leaders and values was a communal survival instrument in the face of dehumanization. White adds:

"Few women who knew the pain of childbirth or who understood the agony and depression that flowed from sexual harassment and exploitation survived without friends, without female company. Few lacked female companions to share escapades and courtship or older women to consult about the vicissitudes of life and marriage. Female slaves were sustained by their group activities. Treated by Southern whites as if they were anything but self-respecting women, many bonded females could forge their own independent definition to which they could relate on the basis of their own notions about what women should be and how they should act."

And Children, Too

This was the culture that Harriet Tubman was born into. At age five her childhood as we think of it ended, and she was rented to a white woman to do full-time domestic labor. The white woman believed in torturing Afrikans every day, and the small Harriet was lashed with a leather whip four times across her face and neck as an introduction before breakfast that first day. Harriet's first escape attempt (i.e., attempted prison break) came when she was seven years old. Seen by the latest settler white woman she had been rented out to, while trying to steal a piece of sugar forbidden to Afrikan children, Harriet outran the white woman and her rawhide whip:

> "By and by when I was almost tuckered out, I came to a great big pig-pen. There was an old sow there, and perhaps eight or ten little pigs. I was too little to climb into it, but I tumbled over the high part and fell in on the ground; I was so beaten out that I could not stir.

> "And I stayed from Friday until the next Tuesday, fighting with those little pigs for the potato peelings and the other scraps that came down in the trough. The old sow would push me away when I tried to get her children's food, and I was awfully afraid of her. By Tuesday I was so starved I knew I had to go back to my mistress. I didn't have anywhere else to go, even though I knew what was coming."

Because attempting to escape was the second-most serious crime, Harriet was whipped senseless by the white man of the house. So, Harriet Tubman had become a full-time productive worker, had become familiar with daily violence and utmost danger, had committed crimes and stolen from white settlers, and had tried to escape or prison break. All by age seven. And this was not exceptional in any way, but common, a story shared by millions of New Afrikans.

Harriet's childhood can't be understood easily by us. Certainly not without uprooting the capitalist myth of children, which is implanted like a barb in our minds. A smarmy, romanticized ideology that children are "precious," "cute," naturally "helpless." Who for their own good must be safely isolated and governed within the nuclear family just like women. Powerlessness and being property is masked by a cloying sentimentality (just as the Southern slavemasters always talked on how much they "loved" their supposedly loyal slaves). Instinctively, children know this.

If Harriet had died at age seven, when she made her first prison break and before she had become a leader, we probably would never have heard about her—but she would have been none the lesser. As a person who was self-supporting, who had integrity, courage, and who fought back against oppressors, Harriet at age seven no less than at age seventy, was all that people should be. You can't be more than that. If her example makes you or me remember how often we've backed down, how much we've lost, that's on us.

Harriet Steps Forward

By age fifteen or sixteen, when she had long since become a field hand, an act of open resistance in support of another New Afrikan almost led to her death. One Fall at harvest time she and other captives were working in the fields. One of farmer Barnett's laborers spaced and slid off to the village store. The euro-settler overseer saw this and ran after him. As did Harriet.

> "When the man was found, the overseer swore that he should be whipped, and called on Harriet, among others, to tie him. She refused, and as the man ran away, she placed herself in the door to stop pursuit. The overseer

caught up a two pound weight from the counter, and
threw it at the fugitive, but it fell short and struck Harriet
a stunning blow on the head."

In fact, Harriet's skull had been fractured, and she would bear
a concave depression where her skull-bone had been crushed
in for the rest of her life. Unconscious, she was brought home to
her parents' shack. In a deep coma at first, Harriet was thought
near death and was bedridden for much of that Fall and early
Winter. Only gradually did she regain some strength, helping
her mother with work for awhile before returning to the pile of
dirty rags on the ground that was her bed. Her injury had also
brought on narcolepsy, and Harriet would fall into a deep sleep
at unpredictable times, even when standing up or walking.

Her act of open resistance had placed her, of course, in added danger. Her owner tried to sell away this rebellious worker
who was also damaged goods. But when he brought prospec-
tive buyers to the shack, Harriet would be lying on the ground
seemingly barely able to stand. And her silence toward the
plantation owner, together with her visible head injury and
narcolepsy, convinced the white settlers that she was now mentally defective, too. Actually, she was thinking sharper than
she ever had. Unable to sell her at any price, Harriet's owner
gave up and she was mostly left alone to recover.

Using deception "to fool ole Massa" was another military
tool in the captive arsenal. However skillful Harriet became at
it under life-or-death pressure, it was simply part of the daily
survival tactics used by captive New Afrikans. Remember that
the most macho pro athletes and capitalistic celebrities of today have never ever in their lives functioned under the kind of
pressure that Harriet dealt with calmly every day.

Harriet's act in stopping the white overseer from catching
a rebellious worker was her true coming out, her joining the
liberation struggle that had been rising all around her. That
night other New Afrikans had also been there; had also been

ordered by the overseer to restrain their brother. Like Harriet, they too refused. Again, she was not unique, but one of a people on the move. Harriet Tubman's coming of age cannot really be understood in isolation.

Increasing Violence and Will

We have to step back a moment and take in the whole sweep of the crisis, as the Black Nation, with increasing violence and will, slowly stood up against the limit of its chains. This was the national crisis that at first deformed the old planter capitalism of the George Washingtons and Thomas Jeffersons. And then destroyed their whole System into the rubble of war. We pick up the larger story from the book *Settlers**:

> "The Northern States had slowly begun abolishing slavery as early as Vermont in 1777, in the hopes that the numbers of Afrikans could be kept down. It was also widely believed by settlers that in small numbers the 'childlike' ex-slaves could be kept docile and easily ruled. The explosive growth of the number of Afrikans held prisoner within the slave system, and the resultant eruptions of Afrikan struggles in all spheres of life, blew this settler illusion away.

> "The Haitian Revolution of 1791 marked a decisive point in the politics of both settler and slave. The news from Santo Domingo that Afrikan prisoners had risen and successfully set up a new nation electrified the entire Western Hemisphere. When it became undeniably true that Afrikan people's armies, under the leadership of a 50-year-old former field hand, had in protracted war

* J. Sakai, *Settlers: Mythology of the White Proletariat from Mayflower to Modern* (Montreal and Oakland: Kersplebedeb and PM Press, 2014).

outmaneuvered and outfought the professional armies of the Old European Powers, the relevancy of the lesson to Amerika was intense. Intense.

"The effect of Haiti's great victory was felt immediately. Haitian slaves forcibly evacuated from that island with their French masters helped spread the word that Revolution and Independence were possible. The new Haitian Republic proudly offered citizenship to any Indians and Afrikans who wanted it, and thousands of free Afrikans emigrated. This great breakthrough stimulated rebellion and the vision of national liberation among the oppressed, while hardening the resolve of settler society to defend their hegemony with the most violent and naked terror.

"The Virginia insurrection led by Gabriel some nine years later, in which thousands of Afrikans were involved, as well as that of Nat Turner in 1831, caused discussions within the Virginia legislature on ending slavery. The 1831 uprising, in which sixty settlers died, so terrified them that public rallies were held in Western Virginia to demand an all-white Virginia. Virginia's Governor Floyd publicly endorsed the total removal of all Afrikans out of the state. If such proposals could be entertained in the heartland of the slave system, we can imagine how popular that must have been among settlers in the Northern States.

"The problem facing the settlers was not limited to potential uprisings on the plantations. Everywhere Afrikan prisoners were pressing beyond the colonial boundaries set for them. The situation became more acute as the developing capitalist economy created trends of urbanization and industrialization. In the early 1800s the Afrikan population of many cities was rising faster than that of Euro-Amerikans. In 1820 Afrikans comprised at least 25% of the total population of Washington, Louisville, Baltimore, and St. Louis; at least 50% of the total population in New Orleans, Richmond, Mobile, and Savannah. The percentage of whites owning slaves was higher in the cities than it was in the countryside. **In cities such as Louisville, Charleston, and Richmond, some 65–75% of all Euro-Amerikan families owned Afrikan slaves.** And the commerce and industry of these cities brought together and educated masses of Afrikan colonial proletarians—in the textile mills, mines, ironworks, docks, railroads, tobacco factories, and so on.

"In such concentrations, Afrikans bent and often broke the bars surrounding them. Increasingly, more and more slaves were no longer under tight control. Illegal grog shops (white-owned, of course) and informal clubs flourished on the back streets. Restrictions on even the daily movements of many slaves faltered in the urban crowds.

"Contemporary white travelers often wrote of how alarmed they were when visiting Southern cities at the large numbers of Afrikans on the streets. One historian writes of New Orleans: 'It was not unusual for slaves to gather on street corners at night ...' Louisville newspaper editorial complained in 1835 that 'Negroes scarcely realize the fact that they are slaves ... insolent, intractable ...'

"It was natural in these urban concentrations that slave escapes (prison breaks) became increasingly common. The Afrikan communities in the cities were also human forests, partially opaque to the eye of the settler, in which escapees from the plantations quietly sought refuge. During one 16 month period in the 1850s the New Orleans settler police arrested 982 'runaway slaves'—**a number equal to approximately 7% of the city's slave population.** In 1837 the Baltimore settler police arrested almost 300 Afrikans as proven or suspected escapees—a number equal to over 9% of that city's slave population.

"And, of course, these are just those who were caught. Many others evaded the settler law enforcement apparatus. Frederick Douglass, we remember, had been a carpenter and shipyard worker in Baltimore before escaping Northward to pursue his agitation. At least 100,000 slaves did escape to the North and Canada during these years.

"**Nor should it be forgotten that some of the largest armed insurrections and conspiracies of the period involved the urban proletariat.** The Gabriel uprising of 1800 was based on the Richmond proletariat (Gabriel himself was a blacksmith, and most of his lieutenants were other skilled workers). So many Afrikans were involved in that planned uprising that one Southern newspaper declared that prosecutions had to be halted lest it bankrupt the Richmond capitalists by causing 'the annihilation of the Blacks in this part of the country.'

Margaret Garner (called Peggy), who killed her own daughter rather than allow the child to be returned to slavery.

"The Charleston Conspiracy of 1822, led by Denmark Vesey (a free carpenter), was an organization of urban proletarians—stevedores, millers, lumberyard workers, blacksmiths, etc. Similarly, the great conspiracy of 1856 was organized among coal mine, mill, and factory workers across Kentucky and Tennessee. In its failure, some 65 Afrikans were killed at Senator Bell's iron works alone. It was particularly alarming to the settlers that those Afrikans who had been given the advantages of urban living, and who had skilled positions, just used their relative mobility to strike at the colonial system all the more effectively."

"Freedom is the Recognition of Necessity"

Young Harriet was part of this rising, and aware, despite the prison culture she grew up in, of the larger events. As the explosive ripple of Nat Turner's Uprising spread, for example, she and other captives would illegally gather at night at the shacks of the few literate "free" New Afrikans. The latter were allowed to buy newspapers, and would read aloud to their sisters and brothers about the trials and the political storm that the Uprising had caused.

In 1849, Harriet heard that she and her brothers were about to be sold South. Harriet saw the life-threatening reality and freed herself to deal with it. She had already lost two sisters and their children, who had been sold South and who would never be found again. If she were to be taken on the chain gangs deeper into the South, into malarial rice plantations or harsh plantation lands being cleared in territory strange to her, her chances of escaping were much less.

Harriet was out of there. Time to jet! She joined the Underground Railroad and escaped. Harriet left behind her husband, who was a "free Negro" and who refused to go. It says it all, doesn't it, that he objected to Harriet's escaping? He who was not in danger of being sold away. John Tubman wasn't willing to risk his privileged status just because his wife was in mortal danger. Hey, he wouldn't go North, and you know he wasn't going further South. You can always get another wife. And he did. Ironically, he should have been more principled, because right after the Civil War he was shot in the back and killed by a white man he had argued with.

Her two brothers tried to escape after hearing the rumors, taking Harriet with them. But that night, without supplies and not knowing where to hide, they decided that the danger of being captured was too great. Forcing Harriet to come along, they gave up and returned "home."

Gathering food, Harriet set out again to escape. Deliberately not telling any of the men, not her husband, not her father, or brothers. Moving alone. "Freedom is the recognition of necessity." She later said that her own thinking had broken through politically in an Amazon way in those few days. She had said to herself:

> "There's two things I've got a right to and these are Death or Liberty. One or the other I mean to have. No one will take me back alive; I shall fight for my liberty, and when the time has come for us to go, the Lord will let them kill me."

In escaping, Harriet was re-defining herself. Not only in relation to Southern slavery and the prison warden who claimed to "own" her. **But in relationship to men & the patriarchal family.** She was constructing herself, creating her new identity as an Amazon. Never again, from that moment on, would Harriet Tubman place herself under the command of men. In politics, war, or daily life. She loved her family, and would return as a guerrilla to rescue as many as she could. However, she was also freeing herself from them.

The Largest Radical Conspiracy in u.s. History

The Underground Railroad when Harriet found it had already been in existence over fifty years. Not only as the largest radical conspiracy in u.s. history, involving many thousands, but as a *major front* of the New Afrikan liberation war. Every war has its own character, its unique unfolding. Spontaneously, the mass revolutionary strategy of the New Afrikan slaves had first been to escape, by any means necessary. Stranded on a strange continent, these trickles and streams of escapees flowed together to create "free" communities of New Afrikans in the North, and in the Indian nations. To be seedbeds from which rebuilding offensives would grow. While at the same time robbing the Slave Power of illegitimate "property" and its already thin sense of security. Weakening the pre-Confederate economy.

We are speaking here of a People's *strategy*, worked out in practice by masses of captives and escapees themselves, of mass movements breaking out of prison camps and across borders. During the settler slaveowners' 1776–1783 War of Independence from the British Empire, there was a great tidal wave of New Afrikans escaping and allying themselves with the British. It is an irony that today white Left organizations name themselves after the settler patriots' organization of that day, the "Committees of Correspondence." For the original "Committees of Correspondence" organized night patrols of white men in the North to intercept and kill escaping Afrikans. Again, the book *Settlers* gives us a true account of this suppressed story:

> "The British, short of troops and laborers, decided to use
> both the Indian nations and the Afrikan slaves to help
> bring down the settler rebels. This was nothing unique;
> the French had extensively used Indian military alliances
> and the British extensively used Afrikan slave recruits
> in their 1756–63 war over North America (called 'The

French & Indian War' in settler history books). But the Euro-Amerikan settlers, sitting on the dynamite of a restive, nationally oppressed Afrikan population, were terrified—and outraged.

"This was the final proof to many settlers of King George III's evil tyranny. An English gentlewoman traveling in the Colonies wrote that popular settler indignation was so great that it stood to unite rebels and Tories again. Tom Paine, in his revolutionary pamphlet *Common Sense*, raged against '... that barbarous and hellish power which hath stirred up Indians and Negroes to destroy us.' But oppressed peoples saw this war as a wonderful contradiction to be exploited in the ranks of the European capitalists.

"Lord Dunmore was Royal Governor of Virginia in name, but ruler over so little that he had to reside aboard a British warship anchored offshore. Urgently needing reinforcements for his outnumbered command, on Nov. 5, 1775, he issued a proclamation that any slaves enlisting in his forces would be freed. Sir Henry Clinton, commander of British forces in North America, later issued an even broader offer:

"'I do most strictly forbid any Person to sell or claim Right over any Negroe, the property of a Rebel, who may claim refuge in any part of this Army; And I do promise to every Negroe who shall desert the Rebel Standard, full security to follow within these Lines, any Occupation which he shall think proper.'

"Could any horn have called more clearly? By the thousands upon thousands, Afrikans struggled to reach British lines. One historian of the Exodus has said: 'The British move was countered by the Americans, who exercised closer vigilance over their slaves, removed the able-bodied to interior places far from the scene of the war, and threatened with dire punishment all who sought to join the enemy. To Negroes attempting to flee to the British the alternatives "Liberty or Death" took on an almost literal meaning. Nevertheless, by land and sea they made their way to the British forces.'

"The war was a disruption to Slave Amerika, a chaotic gap in the European capitalist ranks to be hit hard. Afrikans seized the time—not by the tens or hundreds, but by the many thousands. Amerika shook with the tremors of their movement. The signers of the Declaration of Independence were bitter about their personal losses: Thomas Jefferson lost many of his slaves; Virginia's Governor Benjamin Harrison lost thirty of 'my finest slaves'; William Lee lost sixty-five slaves, and said two of his neighbors 'lost every slave they had in the world'; South Carolina's Arthur Middleton lost fifty slaves.

"Afrikans were writing their own 'Declaration of Independence' by escaping. Many settler patriots tried to appeal to the British forces to exercise European solidarity and expel the Rebel slaves. George Washington had to denounce his own brother for bringing food to the British troops, in a vain effort to coax them into returning the Washington family slaves. Yes, the settler patriots were definitely upset to see some real freedom get loosed upon the land.

"To this day no one really knows how many slaves freed themselves during the war. Georgia settlers were said to have lost over 10,000 slaves, while the number of Afrikan escaped prisoners in South Carolina and Virginia was thought to total well over 50,000. Many, in the disruption of war, passed themselves off as freemen and relocated in other territories, fled to British Florida and Canada, or took refuge in Maroon communities or with the Indian nations. It has been estimated that 100,000 Afrikan prisoners—some 20% of the slave population—freed themselves during the war.

"The thousands of rebellious Afrikans sustained the British war machinery. After all, if the price of refuge from the slavemaster was helping the British throw down the settlers, it was not such a distasteful task. Lord Dunmore had an 'Ethiopian Regiment' of ex-slaves (who went into battle with the motto 'Liberty to Slaves' sewn on their jackets) who helped the British capture and burn Norfolk, Va. on New Years Day, 1776. That must have been sweet, indeed. Everywhere, Afrikans appeared with the British units as soldiers, porters, road-builders, guides, and intelligence agents. Washington declared that unless the slave escapes could be halted the British Army would inexorably grow 'like a snowball in rolling.' ...

"What was primary for the Afrikan masses was a strategic relationship with the British Empire against settler Amerika. To use an Old European power against the Euro-Amerikan settlers—who were the nearest and most immediate enemy—was just common sense to many. **65,000 Afrikans joined the British forces—over ten for every one enlisted in the Continental U.S. ranks** ...

"Even in the ruins of British defeat, the soundness of this viewpoint was born out in practice. While the jubilant Patriots watched the defeated British army evacuate New York City in 1783, some 4,000 Afrikans swarmed aboard the departing ships to escape Amerika. Another 4,000 Afrikans escaped with the British from Savannah, 6,000 from Charleston, and 5,000 escaped aboard British ships prior to the surrender. Did these brothers and sisters 'lose' the war—compared to those still in chains on the plantations?

"Others chose neither to leave nor submit. All during the war Indian and Afrikan guerrillas struck at the settlers. In one case, three hundred Afrikan ex-slaves fought an extended guerrilla campaign against the planters in both Georgia and South Carolina. Originally allied to the British forces, they continued their independent campaign long after the British defeat. They were not overcome until 1786, when their secret fort at Bear Creek was discovered and overwhelmed. This was but one front in the true democratic struggle against Amerika."

When Harriet Tubman reached the first "free" (non-Slavery) city of Philadelphia, she met with William Still, the New Afrikan leader of the Underground Railroad there. Hooked up now, and having a rear base area, Harriet became a self-sufficient "conductor" on the Underground Railroad. Working most of the year as a laborer, cleaning or doing laundry or cutting wood, to support herself and save money for raids in the South. Twice a year, usually in the Spring and Fall, Harriet Tubman would travel hundreds of miles (much of it on foot) infiltrating Slave territory to bring escapees out. She conducted nineteen guerrilla raids, even reaching deep into the Carolina plantation country.

While the Underground Railroad was famous in its own day, especially after being popularized in Harriet Beecher Stowe's best selling novel, *Uncle Tom's Cabin*, in 1852, it was very different than the images of daring white Quakers we are spoon-fed today. **It was mainly composed of New Afrikans, not euro-amerikans. There were many white Abolitionists in the North, but relatively few were willing to risk themselves, or even contribute much money.**

In the South, a handful of "free" Afrikans and Anti-Slavery whites played a key role, but the river of New Afrikan prisoners breaking out was, of course, the largest single part of the Underground Railroad. Most of the "station-masters" and "brakemen" (local Underground Railroad coordinators) were

New Afrikan as well. And when it came to the over five hundred "conductors," those frontline guerrillas who actually penetrated Slave territory to lead prison breaks, virtually all were New Afrikan. It was their war.

We've said it before, but we have to repeat it so that we really get it. The Underground Railroad that Harriet joined in 1849 and came to help lead, wasn't civilian, but a military activity. In fact, it was the *main* Black military activity in their protracted war against the Slave System. It was a mass form of guerrilla warfare. This is the key that opens up an understanding about the nature of war by the oppressed. Which is a level of understanding long denied women, but that we Amazons must break into.

When the capitalist patriarchy praises the Underground Railroad with dusty words, it does so to mislead us. To turn us away from Harriet's own tracks. In our school daze, the Underground Railroad is always falsely praised for being about humanitarian rescue. For being about New Afrikans seeking safety in the white North. As though the Underground were only some Red Cross mission. As though the white North was safe for New Afrikan women. No, not even close to true when we really think about it.

For the Black guerrillas like Harriet the North served as the rear base area in their long war against the Slave System. Rear base areas are little discussed, but essential to guerrillas. This is something precise: a large area or territory, bordering on the main battle zone, where the other side cannot freely operate. Either for reasons of remoteness or impenetrable mountain ranges, or because it crosses political boundaries. The North as a rear base gave New Afrikans the space to rest, repair, and rebuild themselves. This was a deeper process than we've thought about.

In real life, revolutionary guerrillas spend most of their time in rear base areas, not out on raids. In China, Mao Zedong even thought that only one battle every three months was the right spacing for full-time guerrilla units. Because it's in the rear base areas that the process of mass change, of the oppressed changing themselves into new people educationally and politically and classwise and in identity, was centered. So rear base areas were and are not passive, not like highway rest stops. And escaping northward for ex-slaves then wasn't an end in itself, but only a beginning.

The war of liberation was at work just as hard in the Northern rear base area as in the Southern battle zone, although the shape of the activities was clearly different. It is true that relatively few escapees became guerrillas, as Harriet did. Most New Afrikans in the North as *individuals* were largely concerned in their daily lives about finding jobs, caring for children, and all the other difficult demands of survival in Babylon. But as a *community* what they had in common was the liberation war. Their collective efforts, the institutions they built so painfully from nothing in a hostile land, the new leaders they raised up, were all about making war against the Slave System.

Although the white North back then is sentimentally pictured for us as being "the land of freedom," actually it was cold and barren and hostile for New Afrikans. Before the Civil War many towns and even entire states banned New Afrikans as residents, as did almost all skilled trades, professions, hospitals, schools, churches, and government services. To start a primary school for New Afrikan children in most Northern towns then was seen as a shocking crime, and often such small attempts were burned to the ground by angry white mobs. There was nothing Black, no progress or failure, that was not part of the liberation war.

If Harriet Tubman lived in the North, working as a laborer nine or ten months a year during her guerrilla years, this was not a "time-out." If William Still wore a suit and tie and worked as a clerk in Philadelphia during those years, that didn't make him a civilian. He was a major leader of the single largest Eastern station on the Underground Railroad. Every Black

Above: A Freedmen's school, depicted in *Harper's Weekly*.

Below: The burning of a Freedmen's school in Tennesee, also depicted in *Harper's Weekly*.

community association or institution back then was involved in the war. The African Methodist Episcopal Church in lower Manhattan was the first formal New Afrikan church. Formed in a split from a white church that wasn't militant enough for them against slavery. For years it and sister churches through-out the North acted against the law as dissident political centers and as hideouts for fugitive New Afrikans.

Again, the rear base area in the North wasn't a passive refuge but an area of possible advantage and also danger that had to be continually fought for, enlarged, and changed. Which Harriet Tubman was very busy doing all the time. Virtually none of this was recorded in men's history, of course, since the actual fabric of women's politics has always been judged too trivial for that. When Harriet took in poor children in a communal way, urging everyone to construct their households in similar communal fashion, this was a political statement so strong that few women here and now can even discuss it.

While there were already anti-capitalists in the u.s. at that time, Harriet's working-class politics weren't expressed ideologically but in living her New Afrikan communalism. Although she never hid her political view that it was wrong to have any personal wealth or advantage whatsoever.

The constant struggle by Harriet and her comrades to build a New Afrikan culture in the Northern rear base area grew more visible after the passage of the Fugitive Slave Act in 1850. Not only were "slavecatchers" and federal marshals (the

Ann Maria Weems, who escaped the Slave System passing as "Joe Wright" forerunners of today's f.b.i.) seizing escaped Afrikans, but in the shadows of this law white kidnapping of any Afrikans in the North for quick sale on the Southern auction blocks was taking place.

A movement of illegal but open mass resistance arose to the u.s. criminal justice system. A mass movement that rescued New Afrikan prisoners and fought the police and courts and federal marshals. Like all true mass struggles, it had many leaders and many brilliant local battles. One of the most famous then was the Battle of Troy, New York. Which was led by an illiterate working-class woman who was herself a fugitive with a bounty on her head. None other than Harriet Tubman. For you see, in real life, "America's Most Wanted" was a working-class New Afrikan woman.

On April 27, 1860, Harriet Tubman was traveling to Boston to attend a large Anti-Slavery meeting. Stopping in Troy to visit a relative, she was immediately told that a fugitive New Afrikan,

THE FUGITIVE SLAVE LAW IN OPERATION.

Charles Nalle, had been captured by the slavers. Federal marshals were holding him at the downtown courthouse, where his so-called "enslaver" was applying to a u.s. commissioner for Nalle's return in chains back to Virginia. Those at the hearing were surprised, for the thirty-year-old Nalle and the slaver looked strikingly alike, differing only in a shade of skin color. They were biologically two brothers with the same father, but one the captive laborer and one the prison warden. Downtown stores had closed, as everyone was going to the courthouse to see the Roman spectacle.

Harriet had helped quickly organize a conspiracy. With her face hidden in a large shawl, carrying a basket, Harriet bent over acting like an old woman. Two other women were by her side, pretending to support her by the arms. Tugging the guard by his coat, Harriet persuaded him to admit the "harmless" women to the courtroom. Where she sank down in the doorway.

Outside, a New Afrikan man named William Henry started speaking to the crowd, covertly warning some among them to get ready: "There's a fugitive in that office. Pretty soon you will see him come forth … He's going to be taken to the depot to go to Virginia on the first train." Henry, who was an unknown laborer, is believed to be Harriet's brother and the relative she was visiting in Troy.

When the u.s. commissioner ruled against Nalle, the prisoner suddenly leapt for the window and stepped out on the ledge. Cries of support came from below. But his hopes to jump down into the crowd were cut off when Federal agents grabbed him and dragged him back inside. As the local newspaper reported:

> "The crowd at this time numbered nearly a thousand persons. Many were black, and a good share were of the female sex. They blocked up State Street from First Street to the alley, and kept surging to and fro."

Nalle's defense attorney, Martin Townsend, delayed the slavers by filing an emergency appeal right then and there. He won an order demanding Nalle's appearance before a judge of the State Supreme Court. As the slavers and Federal agents convoyed the chained Nalle out, Harriet Tubman rose and threw off her disguise. Racing to the open window, she shouted to the Anti-Slavery fighters mixed in the crowd: "Here he comes! Take him!"

Harriet and her Underground group had arranged for a boat to be secretly waiting at the river outside town. She ran down the courthouse stairs, overtaking the Federal party and breaking into their circle. Locking her arms with Nalle's Harriet began pulling him away from the u.s. marshals. "This man shall not go back to slavery!" she shouted. "Take him, friends! Drag him to the river!"

In the middle of a crowded downtown street, a small battle raged. Federal agents and police swung their clubs, and some drew their pistols and began firing. New Afrikan guerrillas and their white allies charged into them. Nalle himself fought desperately to get free, side by side with Harriet. Attorney Martin Townsend witnessed it all:

> "In the melee she was repeatedly beaten over the head with policemen's clubs, but she never for a moment released her hold, but cheered Nalle and his friends with her voice, and struggled with the officers until they were literally worn out with their exertions, and Nalle was separated from them."

They hurried Nalle down to the river, where a sympathetic ferryman rowed him to the other side. But no sooner had a bloodied and exhausted Nalle touched the shore again than he was recaptured. This time the u.s. marshals and police rushed him under heavy guard to Police Justice Stewart's office, which they barricaded. Just in time, as Harriet had led a rush of four hundred Anti-Slavers on to the steam ferry boat and across the river.

When the u.s. marshals hiding inside started firing wildly at the surrounding force, someone rallied the attackers. "They can only kill a dozen of us—come on!" New Afrikan men charged up the stairs and forced open the door. The first of them was cut down by a hatchet swung by Deputy Sheriff Morrison. His body stuck in the doorway, though, so the door could not be slammed shut. The Anti-Slavery men broke in, but were overcome in hand-to-hand fighting one by one. Then, as Attorney Townsend tells us, it was all on a squad of Black Amazons to win or lose the battle:

> "And when the men who led the assault upon the door of Judge Stewart's office were stricken down, Harriet and a number of other colored women rushed over their bodies, brought Nalle out, and putting him into the first wagon passing, started him for the West."

After the battle u.s. marshals tried to hunt them down, but members of the underground hid them well. And an entire New Afrikan Nation protected Harriet. How shallow is today's false image of Harriet as a lone, non-political do-gooder, when we glimpse her reality as an Amazon leader of an entire people at war. What was happening in the guerrilla war was that violent battles were taking place not only in the South but in the North as well. Thousands upon thousands of New Afrikans created new battlegrounds, and endured the real costs and real casualties of bitter struggles. Women easily as much as men. In that long, difficult, and successful process to develop the North as a vibrant Rear Base Area for their war, women and men stepped up to recreate themselves in dignity. "Freedom is never given, but only won."

Underground Railroad leader William Still gave an example of the militancy of escaping New Afrikans. In 1855, six fugitives breaking out of Virginia complete with the owner's horses and carriage, were stopped on the road by a posse of white patrollers:

"At this juncture, the fugitives verily believing that time had arrived for the practical use of their pistols and dirks, pulled them out of concealment—the young women as well as the young men—and declared they would not be taken! One of the white men raised his gun, pointing the muzzle directly towards one of the young women, with the threat that he would 'shoot', etc. 'Shoot! shoot!! shoot!!!' she exclaimed, with a double barrelled pistol in one hand and a long dirk knife in the other, utterly unterrified and fully ready for a death struggle. The male leader of the fugitives by this time had pulled back the hammers of his pistols, and was about to fire! Their adversaries seeing the weapons, and the unflinching determination on the part of the runaways to stand their ground, 'spill blood, kill, or die,' rather than be taken, very prudently 'sidled over to the other side of the road' ..."

A BOLD STROKE FOR FREEDOM.

"Moses" and "The General"

All this is the larger context in which Harriet Tubman was a part. To blow away the individualistic fiction of Harriet as a lone rescuer or as a Black superwoman takes nothing that is hers away from her. Instead, it frees her in our understanding to be her true self, a New Afrikan woman who was part of the *military and political leadership* in her People's war. While her underground name was "Moses," it was meaningful that both John Brown and Union Army commanders who knew her respectfully called Harriet "the General."

Her second biographer, Earl Conrad, pinpointed the widespread lack of understanding of Harriet Tubman's **military** role, and the real influence she had in the major events leading to the destruction of the Slave Power:

"It has often been said, 'She made nineteen trips into the slave country,' but the meaning of this enormous enterprise has been hidden in the lack of illustration. A trip into the slave territory and the 'kidnapping' of a band of blacks was no less than a military campaign, a raid upon an entrenched and an armed enemy. If it was anything less than a military task then it would not have engaged the attention of such a martial figure as John Brown, as for many years it did. If conducting was not a military assignment then no men would have been hounded, harassed, jailed and wounded, and no lives would have been lost.

"The Underground Railroad era was one of prolonged, small-scale guerrilla warfare between the North and the South, a campaign that, for its activities, was often violent and always perilous. It was so much like guerrilla warfare that it influenced John Brown into the theory that a more extensive development of this type of conflict might be useful as a means of breaking the grip of the slaveholders upon the economy, the politics and the government of the nation; it was one of the longest campaigns of defiance in the nation's history.

"When it is remembered that the Underground was an institution in American life for at least a half century, that by 1850 it was an issue so much at the core of the American problem that called forth an ignominious Fugitive Slave Law, and that it was one of the greatest forces which brought on the Civil War, and thus destroyed slavery, then alone is it possible to comprehend its significance. Harriet Tubman's outstanding participation in the Underground in its last and most vigorous phase, from 1850 until the Civil War, must be approached in the light of such a far-reaching influence as that."

"Free" New Afrikan woman in North being kidnapped to be brought South.
The American Anti-Slavery Almanac, 1836

We have to go more consciously into the question of Harriet's politics. For when Amazons and fighting women appear—as we always will—Patriarchal Capitalism tries to contain us *ideologically*. We are marginalized in one way or another, even if they have to romanticize us as lone exotic super-women. You know, like the talking dog. It isn't what she says that's important, it's that she talks at all that's amazing.

So even when Amazons are supposedly being "honored" it is usually irritating, to say the least. If you saw that wretched television movie about Harriet Tubman, you can catch what i mean. There's elegant Cecily Tyson playing Harriet as some kind of arrogant saint, having to pump up and push ahead the dumb, fearful folks she was freeing. As if Harriet was the only New Afrikan there with any guts. As if Cecily Tyson has anything to do with Harriet. *Again, to take women out of our political context trivializes us.*

Harriet wasn't leading the weak. No, that's got it backwards. She was leading the *strong*. The great Anti-Slavery struggle was a movement of the best and the bravest, the most serious-minded folks of that day. And it was among these, the strong, that Harriet was a leader. She was an Amazon player in the political decisions that determined the ending of the Slavery System.

Harriet did this during the years when she was a wanted fugitive and doing political-military work underground. It wasn't only in the South that her guerrilla activity violated the laws of the u.s. empire. No sooner had she liberated herself than Congress passed the infamous Fugitive Slave Act of 1850, which authorized the hunting of escaped New Afrikan prisoners and wanted revolutionaries all over the North as well. The act paid a special fee to u.s. marshals for handing over accused Afrikans, while it denied the accused any bail or trial in the North.

This unleashed a legion of Southern agents and bounty hunters throughout the country. Harriet and many others had to shift their base of operations. For seven years, Harriet and those of her family she had helped escape lived in exile in St. Catharines, Ontario in Canada. This undeveloped town was one of the first "free" New Afrikan settlements and was much looked to. While whites and Indians lived there as well, to New Afrikans, it was a temporary rear base area. The battle lines had shifted, the North was no longer safe for escaped prisoners, and Harriet used Canada as her rear base to rest up between raids, to take new fugitives to.

Eventually, the Slaveocracy would put bounties totaling $40,000, in 1850s dollars, on Harriet's head. It wasn't her guerrilla raids on their plantations alone that hurt the planter capitalists, but the growing effect of her example to others and her larger political role. Confederates would even point to her later with frustration as one of the causes of the rebellion. On June 1, 1860, for example, feminists gathered in Boston for the annual New England Anti-Slavery Society Conference staged their own "Drawing Room Convention" at Melodeon Hall to discuss women's role in culture. Harriet Tubman was one of the speakers. A newspaper reported the appearance of the wanted Amazon:

> "A colored woman of the name of Moses, who [is] herself a fugitive, has eight times returned to the Slave States for the purpose of rescuing others from bondage, and who has met with extraordinary success in her efforts, won much applause."

The pro-slavery writer John Bell Robinson would single out that day as a special injury to white men's power: "Now I ask all the candid men to look at the congregation of traitors a little, and see if the South had no reason not only to be insulted, but alarmed to the extreme, when they learned that enough such men and women at Melodeon Hall in Boston in 1860, to

densely fill it, and would laugh and shout over such wicked-
ness in a poor weak-minded Negro woman, in trampling upon
the rights of the South with impunity. What could be more
insulting after having lost over $50,000 worth of property by
that deluded Negress, than for a large congregation of whites
and well-educated people of Boston to endorse such an imposi-
tion on the constitutional rights of the slave states."

Fun to laugh at that frustrated white supremacist, but home
in on the fact that even 150 years later women have, in our own
way, as much difficulty accepting Harriet as he did. That's why
the capitalist patriarchy has so easily dis-figured her. Harriet
was a guerrilla not just in the obvious way, but on a deeper
level. We have trouble seeing her as real because she totally
disobeyed the patriarchal and hierarchical rules that *we* still
live by; in which people's lives are strictly bar-coded by dress
and role, race and gender, and, above all, by class.

It's a take on us that the capitalist patriarchy has so easily
conned us into thinking that Harriet was only a goody two-
shoes. When she was an Amazon, and one of the most subversive players in u.s. history. Check us out on that.

Frederick Douglass is considered the preeminent New
Afrikan leader of the 19th century. A brilliant and persuasive
public speaker and writer, Douglass was a towering public figure of that age. But Harriet was no less a leader of her people.
As Douglass himself wrote to her: "I have wrought in the day—
you in the night. I have had the applause of the crowd and the
satisfaction that comes of being approved by the multitude …
The midnight sky and the silent stars have been the witnesses
to your devotion to freedom and your heroism. Excepting John
Brown—of sacred memory—I know of no one who has willingly encountered more perils and hardship to serve an enslaved
people than you have."

While Douglass became a spokesman for the Anti-Slavery
cause, Harriet for years concealed herself and her work as a

guerrilla. What could Douglass' speeches have been without the growth of the Underground Railroad and the mass resistance which Harriet played such a part in building? And in the underground, it was Douglass who was the supporter to Harriet, sheltering in his Rochester, New York, house the fugitives she was leading on the last leg to safety in Canada.

Just as Douglass fits our programmed image of a leader while Harriet does not, Harriet does not register with our patriarchal image of a soldier. Having no official rank or uniform or place in men's hierarchy. Yet & again, she was the first woman to serve in the Union Army, and in retirement kept as her proudest possession the army rifle she had carried in action in the Civil War. While Dr. Martin Delany, the early Black nationalist, is recognized as a soldier for being the first New Afrikan commissioned as a Major in the u.s. army, Harriet had been conducting guerrilla raids on the plantations for over twelve years before there was a Civil War. **Breaking the rules as an Amazon.**

By the end of the 1850s the irresistible progress of New Afrikan liberation had forced the end of the old u.s. and brought the crisis to a head. Where once captive New Afrikans escaped by the ones and twos, now prison breaks were assuming a mass character. In one famous 1857 Maryland prison break, organized by none other than Harriet herself, thirty-nine New Afrikans escaped heavily armed with stolen revolvers, swordcanes, and butcher knives. Women no less than men. Armed resistance was once so shocking when done by Nat Turner and his men in 1831, but was becoming universal.

Harriet herself, despite her secrecy, had become a legend. The plantation owners' hatred of her was expressed not only in bounties and wanted posters, but in public discussion of which torture devices would be used by the would-be captors on her before her slow death. Feeling that the general alarm for Harriet as the South's "Most Wanted" made her capture certain, white abolitionists urged her to retire. With no success. A letter survives written by Colonel Thomas Higginson, the fighting Abolitionist minister who was a supporter of John Brown and who would command a Black regiment in the Civil War, after a visit from Harriet:

> "Dear Mother,
> "...We have the greatest heroine of the age here, Harriet Tubman ... I have known her for some time and mentioned her in speeches once or twice—the slaves call her Moses. She has had a reward of twelve thousand dollars offered for her in Maryland and will probably be burned alive when she is caught, which she probably will be, first or last, as she is going again. She has been in the habit of working in hotels all summer and laying up money for the crusade in the winter. She is jet black and cannot read or write, only *talk*, beside acting ..."

Higginson emphasized "talk" because to those fighting slavery, Harriet's quiet speeches, telling of operations in the South against the Slaveocracy, were electrifying. Harriet was an Amazon spearhead, leading by doing. The Canadian Anti-Slavery Society would send funds for her to pick up at *Frederick Douglass' Paper* in Rochester. So would the Irish Anti-Slavery Society. In Scotland, Elize Wigham of the Glasgow Anti-Slavery Society and other Scots women raised support for her raids.

The greatest tribute to her work was the emergency convention of slave owners in 1857, on the Eastern shore of Maryland, where she had been so active. It was called out of panic, about all the prison breaks that Harriet and many other Black guerrillas were doing. It was the first of the slaver capitalist conventions that would soon lead the Slave States into secession, trying to stop the tide of prison breaks with even tighter slave laws. Along with the re-enslavement of "free" Afrikans, many of whom were suspected of being agents or supporters of the underground. Their self-destructive frenzy of repression was understood to be a signal that the end was nearing. The *Antislavery Standard* newspaper wrote happily:

"The operation of the Underground Railroad on the Maryland border, within the last few years has been so extensive that in some neighborhoods nearly the whole slave population have made their escape, and the convention is a result of the general panic on the part of the owners ..."

A Revolutionary Politic

These special conventions begun in Maryland were important. Facing the death of their social order from internal bleeding, patriarchal capitalists in the one Southern state after another held these assemblies to decide their next move. It was these state conventions that decided to leave the u.s.a. and form a new nation just of their own. Which they named the Confederate States of America. So we can see a direct connection between the steady guerrilla war waged by the Underground Railroad and the determining political events of the day. Harriet herself directly helped precipitate the start of the Civil War. She was at the center of the whirlwind.

By 1857, her presence at key meetings began to be noted. She was usually introduced simply as "Moses" or with a fictitious name. On August 1, 1859, she addressed the New England Colored Citizens Convention opposing Colonization, the popular white plan to resolve their "African Problem" by deporting all Afrikans to an Afrikan colony. Abraham Lincoln and Harriet Beecher Stowe were two of its main backers:

"Miss Harriet Garrison was introduced as one of the most successful conductors on the Underground Railroad. She denounced the Colonization movement, and told a story of a man who sowed onions and garlic on his land to increase his dairy production, but soon found the butter was strong, and would not sell, and so he concluded to sow clover instead. But he soon found the wind had blown the onions and garlic all over his field. Just so, she stated, the white people had got the Negroes here to do their drudgery, and now they were trying to root them out and ship them to Africa. 'But,' she said, 'they can't do it: we're rooted here, and they can't pull us up.' She was much applauded."

Portrayed by the Capitalist Patriarchy as a woman without politics, Harriet was the total opposite. She fought for and lived out the most radical politics of her age. For her to fight at mass New Afrikan meetings against Colonization, which was the main white neo-colonial plan then, was only typical. At a time when most settler Abolitionists expected New Afrikans to remain their inferiors and subordinates, even inside the movement, Harriet joined with Frederick Douglass and others to build New Afrikan-led organizations.

Now, armed New Afrikan resistance to the Slaveocracy way back then in the 19th century has been made retroactively respectable. But it wasn't back then, even in much of the Abolitionist movement. The most famous of the white Abolitionist writers and leaders, William Lloyd Garrison, and his American Anti-Slavery Society, held to the strict doctrine of Christian non-violence and battle by "Moral Suasion" only. The revival meeting speaker and Feminist, Sojourner Truth, crisscrossed the North arguing against those who advocated armed slave resistance. Her verbal skirmishes with Frederick Douglass on the issue of violence were dramatic.

Harriet, who traveled armed with a concealed pistol and had sworn never to be taken alive, was on the most radical edge of freedom "by any means necessary." Feminism was a concept even less acceptable to white society than Abolition back then, but Harriet, as a New Afrikan woman, was always an open Feminist. Not only as an associate of Susan B. Anthony, and one who participated in Feminist conferences into old age. But as an Amazon. She didn't *support* the Warrior, she *was* the Warrior. In fact, never in Harriet's life, once she freed herself, did she put herself under the command of men. A fact never discussed by men. Again, she led by actually living the most radical politics of her age.

It's wrong to think of Harriet's politics in civilian terms, because she wasn't a civilian and that wasn't her frame of reference. Her entire life she had been at war. Moreover, Harriet had grasped the main line that led into the future: that the Anti-Slavery struggle was inevitably growing towards all-out war, and only in such total conflict could the issue of her people's enslavement be finally resolved.

To Develop Armed Struggle

As the settler political parties, including the new Anti-Slavery party, the Republicans, vacillated and tried to compromise to avoid secession, Harriet moved and moved others to develop armed struggle. *"They may say 'peace, peace!' as much as they like: I know there's going to be war!"* Harriet said in one of her most famous statements. Her political-military work was like an arrow on a direct and one-way journey towards ever greater armed conflict. Each successively larger wave of the struggle saw her on the leading edge.

In 1858, Harriet Tubman joined John Brown's conspiracy to start a permanent guerrilla army inside the South. Her friend Frederick Douglass arranged for the Rev. J.W. Loguen, one of the leaders of the New Afrikan community in Syracuse, N.Y., and a well-known Abolitionist, to take Brown to meet with Harriet in St. Catharines, Ontario. Brown stayed on as Harriet's guest in her house for some days, discussing the plan.

Harriet's participation in this attempt brings us to the edge of a deeper understanding. We are always told that John

Brown's conspiracy was the brave but hopeless gamble by a small handful of zealots. Why, then, was Harriet so eagerly involved? She was, after all, herself the veteran of ten years of guerrilla warfare. Someone who rarely in the war zone put her foot down wrong. Intensely practical.

The answer is that while Brown's last minute decision to seize the Federal Arsenal at Harpers Ferry, W. Virginia, in order to publicize the campaign, was a poor decision and poorly executed, their overall strategy was both simple and practical. It received serious discussion among many of the leading New Afrikan activists of the day. It was a logical next step.

Brown had envisioned a small guerrilla force, roaming up and down the length of the Allegheny Mountains, sheltered in its terrain. Harpers Ferry, W.E.B. DuBois said, was a natural entry point to the Alleghenys, and thus to the mountains running further to the South. Like a tapeworm growing within the Slave States, this army would come down and raid the plantations of Virginia and the Carolinas in lightning strikes. Constantly growing by the recruiting of freed New Afrikans, while sending larger streams of escapees North via the Underground Railroad.

A secret convention was held May 8, 1858, in Chatham, Ontario, home to the largest Black community in Canada. There a group of thirty-three New Afrikans and twelve euro-amerikans approved the guerrilla army and its constitution. There were New Afrikan men such as the Nationalist and physician, Dr. Martin Delany, the prominent Baptist minister, W.C. Monroe, the Underground Railroad leader G.J. Reynolds, the gunsmith and Oberlin college graduate, James Jones, and James Harris, the future u.s. congressman from North Carolina.

Brown's dangerous attempt received so much interest because it was an idea whose time had come. This was the next higher stage in the struggle. One that years of growing prison breaks and violent resistance had made inevitable. If the Civil

War and Lincoln's Emancipation Proclamation had never happened, the capitalist Slave System would have been crushed nevertheless. The idea that New Afrikans would soon free themselves in a major war was one that was common at the time.

Wendell Phillips, Garrison's brilliant associate in the American Anti-Slavery Society, publicly linked John Brown to this expectation of New Afrikan self-determination. Before a crowd of thousands he praised "… the spirit, that looks upon the Negro as a Nation, with the right to take arms into its hands and summon its friends to its side, and that looks upon that gibbet of John Brown, not as a scaffold of a felon but as the cross of a martyr."

Brown's plan had actually grown out of the experience of Harriet and other conductors, who used the Allegheny Mountains as a guerrilla highway. He saw the Underground Railroad as the other half to his small army, bringing supplies and communications from the North while it was an outer network of intelligence and propaganda ahead of his mobile force. Of course, Brown knew far less of the ground he proposed to fight on than Harriet.

John Brown

So we can understand how important Harriet's participation was to him. After meeting her he wrote to his son: "I am succeeding to all appearance, beyond my expectation. Harriet Tubman hooked on his whole team at once. He is the most man, naturally, that I ever met with …"

46

This Wasn't Just About Race

Brown's pen, in his fervor, suddenly had to jump-cross genders, as he had no words for women sufficient to express his admiration. Which opens the door for us. John Brown was, of course, a patriarch, in his own eyes even. Important affairs were manly affairs, to him. At the Chatham secret convention, a New Afrikan man proposed recruiting women to the conspiracy. Brown strongly opposed this, and according to one participant "warned the members not to intimate, even to their wives, what was done."

So even back then it was necessary for men to exceptionalize Harriet. John Brown's conspiracy and armed band were all male, by deliberate intention. Yet, perhaps the single most crucial person and guerrilla they needed was a New Afrikan woman, and Amazon. It's easy to see how John Brown had to redefine Harriet as a "man" in his mind. And thought that his supreme compliment, too.

From women's point of view, John Brown's campaign and the secret men's convention in Canada are like an x-ray into real politics. Weren't we always taught subliminally that only white men had serious politics & serious political debates? Yet & again, the Anti-Slavery movement in Harriet's time seethed with the contradictory visions of nationhood, race, and gender. Then, as right now, these were only the outward forms that deeper class politics took on.

When Harriet Tubman, Dr. Martin Delany, and John Brown came together in Canada that season, there was a life-or-death unity between them. There were also intense class differences moving just beneath the surface. John Brown had called his secret men's convention to hammer out a "Provisional Constitution of the Oppressed People of the United States." His conspiracy needed such a rule, because questions of national strategies and allegiances were in the air. This wasn't just about race.

The Brown expedition was a Black guerrilla nation in its intention. Their goal was not to make raids or free some captives, but to create a sovereign nation—just as in living memory some other men had started the u.s.a. as a brand-new nation This is why they needed a "provisional constitution." The one they drafted, although written solely by men, guaranteed voting rights to women as well as men. Even encouraged all women to arm themselves.

This was at a time when new capitalist men's nations were *being created* all over the world. Both in the decay of old pre-industrial empires and in new anti-colonial struggles. After all, the u.s.a. was a new settler nation itself. People could see that making nations or wiping out nations was just the ordinary work of politics. Same with us, sis.

Everyone then had heard of Toussaint L'Ouverture, who had come to be called the "Black Napoleon." After he had led the 1791 Haitian Revolution, and set up the first self-governing Black nation in the Western Hemisphere. Just as Mexican landowners had ended Spanish colonial rule in 1821, creating a new Mexican nation. And in 1836 euro-amerikan "pioneers" led a war of secession against that new Mexican nation, founding their own, independent slaveowner nation of the Republic of Texas (which later joined the u.s.a. as a state). So leaving nations and constructing nations were much on people's minds then.

If John Brown's guerrilla army had been successful, it would have been like the Maroon colonies of fugitive Afrikans. These colonies and camps had sprung up not only in Jamaica and Brazil, in Central Amerika, but in Southern u.s. swamps and forests, too. By their very nature they were self-governing communities, outside of all colonialist laws & government. For that reason, John Brown felt it important to aim the rebellion's ultimate loyalty to the new United States. They would have no goal other than to "Amend & Reform" the u.s. constitution. They would have no flag, he declared, other than the "Stars and Stripes" itself.

One New Afrikan immediately spoke up at the convention, saying that as an ex-slave he owed no allegiance to the flag of slavery. "The old flag is good enough for me," Brown replied. "Under it, freedom was won from the tyrants of the old world, for white men. Now I intend to make it do duty for Black men." Revealing words.

Dr. Martin Delany spoke up to support Brown, and to favorably move the question of his proposed constitution. But Delany did so with his own nationalist slant, stressing the political & social separatism of the future New Afrikan community: "The independent community that Captain Brown proposes to establish will be similar to the Cherokee Nation of Indians or the Mormons in Utah territory."

See, there were a number of self-governing societies then on the fringes of the territory claimed by the u.s. settler empire. Years before, the adventuresome Delany had crossed the Slave South alone to the Texas frontier, looking for a land that New Afrikans might emigrate to away from settler society. With a horse lent him by the Choctaw, he had ridden through the Choctaw and Chickasaw Nations as a guest. What is now the state of Oklahoma was then named the Indian Territory, set aside by u.s. law for the Native nations expelled from the Southeast in the 1830s.

Dr. Delany had been impressed that the Choctaw had still kept their own society even under euro-capitalist rule. Their nation still retained a semi-autonomous status. Not only did they have their own territory and economy, however poor it was, but their own schools and language, their own laws & court system. Their leaders were recognized in Washington as the diplomatic representatives of another sovereign people. In Dr. Delany's eyes such a semi-autonomous status would be a big transitional step upward for four million New Afrikans, almost all of whom were still en-slaved.

Harriet and Dr. Martin Delany were a contrast. She had been captive for 29 years, born a slave, while he had been born a "free Negro" and come of age in the North. She was working-class, and unable to even read the bible. He was a pioneering Black middle-class professional. One who through persever-ance found white sponsors to learn medicine & even spend a year at Harvard medical school. And while Harriet's politi-cal work was in the South as a guerrilla, Dr. Delany's political work was as an intellectual in the North.

Dr. Delany was one of the very first Pan-Afrikanist educa-tors, and his imprint is still on the politics of the Black Nation. While working in Pittsburg as a cutter (a lay healer who bled blood from the ill, a much prescribed remedy back then) he started what was at the time the only Black Anti-Slavery news-paper in the country. Then, Frederick Douglass recruited him to help publish his famous newspaper, *The North Star.* Dr. Martin Delany even tried becoming a novelist, writing the first Black radical novel, *Blake.* The story of an international conspiracy of the en-slaved that finally seizes Cuba, *Blake* was the first New Afrikan book advocating revolution and denouncing whites as a race. And it ends with the angry words, "Woe be unto these devils of whites, I say."

Dr. Delany was a forerunner, an early nationalist whose work helped inspire W.E.B. DuBois, the Nation of Islam, and other groups. He understood that New Afrikans were a colo-nized nation: "We are a nation within a nation—as the Poles in Russia, the Hungarians in Austria; the Welsh, Irish, and Scotch in the British dominions."

Along with Rev. Henry Highland Garnett, the militant pas-tor, Delany was one of the first advocates of Afrikan nationalist migration. Although he agreed that Black people were u.s. citi-zens and should fight for all their rights here, Delany proudly argued that his people deserved an "even better" development of their own society and their own leadership. White society would never offer them justice in any case, he said.

He advocated initial Afrikan settlements in Central America and the Caribbean, to learn from, before migration back to

Afrika. In his pioneering expedition to Nigeria he gathered examples of Afrikan products and signed a commercial treaty with an Afrikan chief. Wearing Afrikan robes, Dr. Delany toured the North after his return, telling fascinated Black audiences hungry for news from Afrika about the societies and economic potential he had seen.

There's no question that Dr. Delany made significant contributions to radical Black self-assertion. We need to explore these gender and class differences not to diminish anyone, but to illuminate the meaning of the choices people made. Because Dr. Martin Delany is used to dis Harriet. Men have come to imply and assume what a recent, much-acclaimed "history of African-American literature," Dr. Eric J. Sunquist's *To Wake the Nations*,* explicitly states: that Dr. Martin Delany was one of the great founders of the Black "revolutionary" viewpoint, while Harriet Tubman is dismissed as "less militant." Outside of the obvious, that it's just like men to decide that the most brilliant guerrilla leader this side of Geronimo was "less militant" than her male compatriots, there's a poisoned idea implanted here. Dr. Delany is implied to be the more political one, the mover, while once again women are implied to be only supporters and doers of tasks. Although in Harriet's case the little woman's task was destroying the Confederacy and its whole system.

The unexplored political difference between Harriet and Dr. Martin Delany was a gender difference. Which is a class difference. They represented and tried to give leadership to different classes in the Black Nation. They had different ideas on what the Black community should become, with Harriet's ideas being the more radical & the more Afrikan.

It was no coincidence that Dr. Martin Delany was inside the Chatham convention reaching agreements with John Brown, while Harriet & all other women were out in the cold. Just cause and effect, girl. Just the inescapable gravitational pull

---

* Published by Harvard University Press in 1993.

of gender & class. Stick with us here, we have to detour some through these men's politics. Because they are the background to see Harriet's own course.

John Brown's politics there carried the internal contradictions of u.s. anti-racism. Contradictions still alive right now. If successful, the conspirators would have created a guerrilla liberated zone in the Southern mountains, one in which New Afrikans would be a self-governing people totally outside u.s. control. Yet & again, Brown was an amerikkkan patriot, a small businessman who believed in the sacred cause of the u.s.a. as a god-given land for white men & their Black brothers. The unity containing these violent opposites was an unconscious neo-colonialism. His "Provisional Constitution of the Oppressed People ..." committed New Afrikan rebels to not even overthrow any Southern state governments, but only to "Amend & Reform" the u.s. constitution to end chattel slavery. John Brown, who so willingly gave his own life and his sons' lives for justice, also simply assumed as natural a patriarchal capitalist hierarchy to life. That's why he was "Commander-In-Chief" over Black men, and New Afrikan women not even allowed in the room when political decisions were being made.

To Brown and Delany, women were still the led, the governed. That Dr. Martin Delany himself envisioned a male ruling class is clear. As he said in his famous slogan: "Africa for the African people, and Black men to rule them."

Gradually, we have drawn Harriet and Martin together in our story, side by side, so that we can catch the meaning that existed in their relationship. From different origins their lives came to cross each other's, and then to separate. Both lived in log cabins in the hard Canadian exile communities in the 1850s. They were even neighbors, in nearby towns, who knew of each other as comrades in their rising freedom struggle.

Yet and again, Harriet and Martin were also profoundly alien to each other, the working-class Amazon and the entrepreneurial patriarchal nationalist. Magnetic polar opposites in the developing gender-class contradictions. For Harriet and Martin stood on opposite sides of a rapidly growing divide in the world, engulfed in the explosive onrush of a world class struggle.

For the Black Nation, you see, was not apart from world politics, not apart from world history. So often patriarchal capitalism gives us a post-surgical kind of Black history that seems to be just about itself. That pretends to exist in a little history bubble, separate from the rest of the human race's story.

But Harriet and Martin's time was also the time when the world was first welded together under an industrial euro-capitalist rule. While they were building their Canadian rear base area, Commodore Perry's u.s. navy "black fleet" was bombarding Japan and forcing the shoguns to accept u.s. trade. A time when predatory industrial ecology and white settlerism were removing the Indian Nations ever westward, on ever shrinking patches of ground, until the survivors of u.s. genocide became small communities of prisoners. A time when Black Afrika was being investigated and mapped for european colonial armies arriving and soon to come.

A time when in numerous indigenous societies of Asia, Afrika, and the Western hemisphere, women, as a people unto ourselves with our own economic power, our own self-rule, our own mystery, were broken by capitalist colonialism into isolated individual "pieces" and assigned to the nuclear family of man.

It was no accident that Dr. Delany was being applauded at a gathering of the Royal Society in London, signing commercial treaties in Nigeria, and publishing books. While Harriet was a fugitive conducting protracted, long-range guerrilla raids on the plantation prisons to free New Afrikan prisoners. They were both caught up in what we can now see was a global class struggle, of the malignantly expanding euro-capitalism on one side against indigenous communalistic cultures on the other. A gender-class divide that would razor through the heart of the Black Nation.

Dr. Martin Delany's dreams were male dreams, of Black capitalistic men rising to join their european brothers in building new commercial empires and nations. He had an honest vision, of the elite of Black men mobilizing themselves to be a proud part of a "man's world." Hand in hand with their white partners, Delany's vision saw the most ambitious New Afrikan men becoming indispensable equals with the european powers in exploiting the great mineral wealth, labor, and trade of Black Afrika. Not enemies at all for Martin, but male partners.

So while men have pointed to Dr. Martin Delany as a revolutionary model of anti-white defiance, his actual politics were much more complex. His vision of Black independence had a closely constructed capitalism of class and gender. In his most famous writing, *The Condition, Elevation, Emigration and Destiny of the Colored People of the United States*, Martin called for "an Expedition of Adventure to the Eastern Coast of Africa." The large funding necessary to in effect take over East Afrika, and establish a ruling nation of Western-educated Black emigrants from the u.s., he amazingly believed would be given to them by the British and French empires:

> "... To England and France, we should look for sustenance, and the people of those two nations—as they would have everything to gain from such an adventure and eventual settlement on the EASTERN COAST OF AFRICA— the opening of an immense trade being the consequence. The whole Continent is rich in minerals, and the most precious metals ... with a settlement of enlightened freemen, who with the immense facilities, must soon grow into a powerful nation."

What was most chilling to me about his words was the unconscious implication that East Afrika then was empty, wide open territory for any band of capitalist men who decided to settle there and start their own nation. Isn't this so achingly familiar? Like the "empty" North Amerika that euro-capitalism gave itself the right to move into, settle, fill up, cleanse. Weren't there existing Afrikan societies already there, then? Existing masses of women, children, and men? What rights or role would those native societies have had? Or would they have unintentionally been the equivalent to Indians in the final working out of Martin's capitalistic vision?

This guy-think is really typical for all patriarchal capitalism. Even the Black separatism of that day. The seductive illusion that there can be a benign, "good" capitalism if done by the formerly oppressed, is just that. Martin's nationalistic colleague, the Rev. Henry Highland Garnett, and his African Civilization Society, argued for emigration back to Afrika on a program of defeating the South with Black capitalism.

Challenged by Garnett to debate emigration, Frederick Douglass repeated their program with dry sarcasm:

> "The African Civilization Society says to us, go to Africa, raise cotton, civilize the natives, become planters, merchants, compete with the Slave States in the Liverpool cotton market, and thus break down American slavery."

Left unspoken was the obvious question of how anyone could undercut the price of Southern cotton produced by unpaid imprisoned labor. That's even if introducing the capitalism of cotton plantations, planters and all, to Afrika would have been anything less than a eurocentric home invasion. Even if, or especially if, it were done by some Black men themselves. Dr. Martin Delany's own Black migration strategy was a plan for the rise of a small New Afrikan bourgeois male class. Logistically not even all the clipper ships in the world could have moved four million New Afrikans back to Afrika faster than their population increase. To say nothing of where millions of Black laborers in a place they'd never been might obtain huge tracts of farmland, tools, supplies. No, Dr. Delany's actual plans were for the small migration of Black businessmen, who would become Afrika's Western educated merchants, plantation owners & entrepreneurs. The middlemen selling Afrika's handicrafts, agricultural products, and minerals to the world.

The reality about such well-intentioned male nationalist dreams was that underneath the surface layer of seeming practicality, of self-assured guy-talk about the man's world of power economics and power politics, their plans were really naive and impractical. Brilliant and serious as Martin was, he wasn't even close to the ball park. Dr. Delany and Rev. Henry Highland Garnett and their associates inwardly assumed the basic neutrality of capitalism. That men would always want to play ball with men. In real life, of course, capitalism doesn't play. After the Civil War, the Black men's trading venture with Afrika that Dr. Delany started went bankrupt after their hired sea captain defrauded them in order to pick their ship up cheaply for himself at bankruptcy auction.

While in the bigger picture, world capitalism was entering its stage of high imperialism and colonial empire monopolies. Britain and France didn't need Dr. Martin Delany at all to enrich themselves on Afrika. His plans at best were an anachronism from earlier centuries. The european colonial powers threw themselves into "the scramble for Africa," which ended with Britain, France, Germany, Portugal, Spain, Belgium, and Italy invading and almost completely dividing up the Afrikan continent, its ecology and peoples, among themselves by 1895. Millions of Afrikans there were captives and semi-slaves in the new capitalist mines, plantations, highway projects. Millions were dying from starvation and brutality. Dr. Delany had long since been frozen out of Nigeria, his treaty torn up under British orders. Afrikan emigration, while exploring a militant rejection of u.s. injustice, was a dead end.

Even more to the point, it was a class plan for only a small minority of the "best & brightest." This did not go unnoticed by other New Afrikans. In 1860, the newly-elected Abraham Lincoln found his Union dissolving. The Southern states were seceding even before his Inauguration. The new President tried to calm settler fears about possible masses of freed New Afrikans by picking up Dr. Delany's own plan for Central American settlements. He promised that as quickly as New Afrikans were "freed" they would be deported. The Lincoln administration and Congress appropriated funds to establish a colony for ex-captives in Panama. Overwhelmingly, the Anti-Slavery movement attacked Lincoln playing the Black colony card as a racist move. To get rid of the Black community's boldest & most resourceful, potential leaders, as well as divide their people just as the Crisis was upon them. A few, notably the nationalist forerunner Rev. Henry Highland Garnett, did support Lincoln. Dr. Delany, on lecture tour in the West, wasn't in the debate.

It is true that Harriet was not a public leader and writer in the way that Frederick Douglass and Dr. Martin Delany were. It's also true that these debates among "free Negroes" in the North were only in the periphery of her vision. Harriet was focussed on guerrilla war in the South. Where the great majority of her people still were, workers & laborers just as Harriet was, isolated and in chains. She always likened Slavery to being literally in Hell, and her attention was concentrated on the immediacy of jailbreaking her people out of Hell. An Amazon warrior, she was busy at war.

While Dr. Martin Delany's vision of Black businessmen building a new nation empire in Afrika won him lasting recognition, Harriet had no such vision that history has recognized. For Harriet had no politics that men would recognize as politics then or now. Not having a political party or a written doctrine or a plan for hierarchical government. Strong as her politics were, they existed hidden in different form. Of the three leaders whose paths came together then in Canada—John Brown, Dr. Martin Delany, and Harriet Tubman—it was Harriet who had the most rooted vision. For hers was a radical, people-centered way of life that in and of itself stood in warlike opposition to the madness of capitalism. This is important to us, and we'll come back to it later.

The New Afrikan volunteers that Harriet & Dr. Martin Delany had recruited, working together in the Canadian exile communities, drifted away to other activities. Delany himself left on a pioneering Pan-Afrikanist expedition to Nigeria. By the time the Harpers Ferry raid finally took place over a year later, Harriet had been taken ill while traveling & was out of contact with John Brown.

Sympathetic historians have always been at pains to stress how Harriet had unexpectedly been brought down by sickness, as though her absence at Harpers Ferry somehow needed explaining. The plain truth was that Harriet wasn't spending her life waiting around for white men to get it together. She had her own guerrilla work, her own political agenda, and she was pursuing those while the dedicated but disorganized John Brown was figuring out what to do. She wasn't the supporter, remember, she was the warrior and leader herself. Even as strong a personality as John Brown couldn't make her into a follower. Harriet raises for us the question of what it means to be an Amazon, to unite the questions of culture and war into your own life and body.

A New Afrikan Political-Military Leader

Harriet's involvement with the failed John Brown conspiracy in 1858–59 signaled a shift.* She moved into a different period, in which her guerrilla work merged into the larger & more

* John Brown's plans were upset right after he returned from Canada in that May of 1858. In your typical case of male bonding, Brown had hired a european military mercenary to give his band some of that male military expertise. The mercenary decided the best strategy would be to betray the conspiracy and sell his story to the highest bidder. There was panic among Brown's wealthy New England backers, and the conspirators had to lie low and postpone everything. Many thought the plan was dead.

open clash that would be the Civil War. But these armies were settler men's organizations. The Union Army was purely a patriarchal and hierarchical structure. And Harriet Tubman was an Outsider, biologically marked in race & gender as one of amerikkka's subject proletarians. But if we ask what Harriet did with the Union Army, the truest answer might be: anything she wanted.

To get this we have to sidestep a moment in our story, shaking off our indoctrination even more & refocusing on Harriet's real life as an Amazon. Harriet's singular characteristic wasn't bravery, as we're always told. That's another sly put-down of women. After all, many other New Afrikan women had also resisted in every way. Took part in prison breaks. Died under torture after attacking settlers. Took part in the Civil War. No, courage was as common as blood to those sisters.

What so distinguished Harriet was that she was a pro. She was one of the most brilliant professional practitioners ever at the art of war. As a guerrilla, so elusive that she could strike fatal blows and never be felt. Lead battles and go unseen. As an Amazon, she conducted warfare in a zone beyond men's comprehension. But her blows still fell on point.

Her professional skill as a guerrilla, operating behind enemy lines in the Underground Railroad, is well documented. Season after season, in nineteen raids, she evaded & misdirected the Slaveocracy. Her always changing tactics were like textbook lessons. Coming under suspicion, she would lead her escapees with forged papers onto a train going South, not North, then circle back. Disguises were sometimes used, disguising women as men or vice-versa. Something Harriet herself did. Once, knowing she might meet her former prison-warden in town, she dressed even more raggedy. And she carried an armful of live chickens. When she saw him, she "accidentally" let the birds loose. Her former prison-warden passed by in amusement at the apparently hapless old Black woman—her face averted as she scrambled on the ground to catch her chickens.

Other times, when a slave would weaken during the difficult journey & want to go back, Harriet would simply put her pistol to his head and give him her only choices: "Dead niggers tell no tales." What i'm saying is, she could walk that walk.

Harriet never put down her personal thoughts, her story as she saw it. She lived in a more personally reticent and cautious age, when women were far less open in proclaiming their personal tactics & strategies. An illiterate ex-slave woman in a hostile land, her only surviving autobiographical accounts were additionally filtered through the motives of interviewers for largely white audiences. No matter how well-intentioned.

The reason we need to be reminded is that Harriet couldn't leave any direct words. Like all those countless sisters lost in history. To counteract the capitalist patriarchy's whiteout of her identity. Unlike, for example, Malcolm X. We have to look at the trail signs she left in the forest of herstory, where her footsteps led. The improbable picture given out now of Harriet is someone who was a bold opponent & tormentor towards the white settlers of the South, but who was a simple, loyal, political go-along towards the white settlers of the North. When we put it that way, how likely is that? Truth was, Harriet had a guerrilla relationship towards all of white amerikkka, North and South. She had, in a deeper sense, an Amazon guerrilla relationship to the Union Army itself.

Harriet, who never hid being a feminist, did not challenge the patriarchal military institutions to end "discrimination." Nor did she put on men's uniforms and try to pass in a regiment. She wasn't trying to be admitted to West Point or get white men's permission to become a soldier. She already was one. Harriet was in a hurry and she wasn't aiming to be a rifle-carrier in a settler men's army. Her aim was far beyond that. As a New Afrikan political-military leader her aim was on the actual mass liberating, arming, and organizing of her people. While doing this she also aimed to assist, prod, guide, and at times even lead, the huge but often clueless Union Army and its white men's government into smashing the Slave States into the dust. This was a military role so ambitious that it seems inconceivable to us. Who are conditioned into accepting the horizons patriarchy permits us. Yet & again, that is precisely what Harriet did.

Even as the new Republican Party president, Abraham Lincoln, was taking office in March 1861, eleven Slave States were seceding & forming their "Confederate States of America." Their gathering Confederate armies threatened Washington, d.c. itself, which was only a Southern Slavery city sandwiched between the two Slave States of Virginia and Maryland. Lincoln called for white volunteers nationwide, and ordered regular Federal troops from the North, under Gen. Benjamin Butler, down to defend the capital.

As Butler's forces moved slowly on foot through Maryland, New Afrikan captives began escaping from plantations and taking refuge with the Union Army. According to William Wells Brown, an ex-slave himself and Underground Railroad worker who spoke with Harriet after the War, she was unofficially on the scene. Harriet had hurried down from her hideout in Canada & just attached herself to the army. As her biographer, Earl Conrad, says:

> "Harriet followed Gen. Butler's army as it marched
> through Maryland on the way to the defense of
> Washington during the months of April and May, 1861,
> when Maryland debated whether to secede and when
> the Federal troops met with violence at Baltimore. It
> was, after all, her home country; she knew how to get in
> and out of here speedily, and she had friends who could
> shelter her. It was an opportunity to stimulate slaves
> to escape to the Union Army or to take care of them as
> rapidly as they came into the Federal camps ... Harriet,
> 'hanging upon the outskirts of the Union Army', was pos-
> sibly the first American woman to visit or work on the
> battlefields of the Civil War."

It was to be in the military theater of the deeper South, however, that Harriet's work with the Union Army was to reach full impact. The Summer and Fall of 1861 were frustrating months of sporadic clashes in Virginia, of Union setbacks, of gathering forces. Radical Abolitionists and New Afrikans were critical of the white-supremacist Lincoln, who was unwilling to either legally end slavery or arm New Afrikans. His first commander, Gen. McClellan, hated Blacks and publicly promised that his troops would join the plantation capitalists to "crush" any Black uprising. Harriet, temporarily back in New England, publicly scorned the settler hopes that by compromising the white family feud could be healed. "Never wound a snake, but kill it!" she warned.

A Nodal Point: Blowing Away the Whiteness

Then, in the Winter, came the news of the Union victory at Port Royal Harbor, South Carolina. Carried by the blockading Union Navy, Federal troops seized the rich plantations of the Sea Islands off the Carolina Coast, Hilton Head, and, on December 8, 1861, the mainland town of Beaufort, S.C. Thousands of formerly en-slaved saw the white settlers fleeing for the interior. While thousands of other New Afrikans would make their way through the forests and swamps and Confederate troops to reach this Union-held territory in the Deep South. Or die trying.

The importance of this victory was much greater than it has appeared. While attention has always been fixed on the main dueling armies—the Union's Army of the Potomac & Robert E. Lee's Army of Northern Virginia—the process that would eventually doom the Confederacy first emerged in the Deep South. That was the Black regiments, inexhaustibly growing as they drew on the millions of the Black Nation. Harriet was right there, one of the military participants & a player in the creation of her people's military strength.

All this has been whited-out, of course, by the capitalist patriarchy. It is laid down for us that "Harriet Tubman was a nurse and spy for the Union Army." While technically not a lie, this is deliberately misleading. First place: we automatically, when we hear the word "nurse," picture a nice, respectable civilian profession, with lots of humanitarian white women nurturing the wounded. Not true. At that time in amerikkka, nursing with an army was a male *military* role. Nursing in general wasn't a profession, and women didn't yet do it.

It was a soldier's job and a "male" role. So much so that, as feminist herstorian Drew Gilpin Faust points out, the few Southern women volunteering as Confederate Army nurses were ...

> "... subjects of gossip and speculation. Women working in hospitals seemed in the eyes of many southerners to display curiously masculine strengths and abilities. Clara MacLean confided to her diary that her neighbor Eliza McKee, recently departed for Virginia as a nurse, had always possessed such strength as to seem 'almost masculine—Indeed I used to tell her I never felt easy in her society if discussing delicate subjects; I could scarcely persuade myself that she was not in disguise.' And Mary Chestnut, the famed South Carolina diarist, felt much the same about the intimidating strength of her friend McCord [nurse Eliza McCord], who seemed to possess 'the intellect of a man.' Nurses were not truly women, but in some sense men in drag."

Harriet was an outsider to those white gender restrictions, since New Afrikan women were not considered "real" women any more than butches were. And she didn't work in any sterile hospitals. There were no MASH units, no antibiotics, no IV drips, no plasma, neither sophisticated surgery nor protective gloves, no medivac out of there. Standard military nursing then was mostly bringing food and water, and cleaning up the blood and dirt and shit. With lots of danger from infectious diseases.

So you'd better believe that Harriet wasn't hanging out on the New Afrikan ward with crowds of white civilian women. Nor was it some minor "helping" role she created.

Again, what we find is that *exceptionalizing* Harriet, making her this individualistic super-woman torn out of her political context, pretends to honor her but actually trivializes her. We were given this picture of heroic Harriet, the lone Black woman nurse and spy, helping out at the side of the gigantic white men's Union Army. Seen that way, her deeds were brave, of course, but insignificant to the real deal, the big bloody battles between settler men's armies that would determine her people's fate. Isn't that the impression we were slyly poisoned with? As though a New Afrikan Amazon could only be a "helper" at the side of the big boys?

Placing Harriet back into her politics, back into her people's struggle, totally changes our understanding of what she was doing. The capitalist patriarchy loves to describe Harriet's army duty as nursing, because it civilianizes her. Since we associate nursing with nurturing & maternal care of white men, it redefines her as a loyal woman to patriarchy. When actually she was subversive to the core.

Harriet wasn't helping a white army, although that's the impression given us. In the Civil War, Harriet was a woman warrior in a Black army. Just as Harriet was not the only New Afrikan woman who took weapon in hand against the planter capitalists, just as she was not the only New Afrikan child who rebelled, so she was not the only Black woman warrior by far. She was one of many, there at the creation.

We know that other New Afrikan women fought. Like Maria Lewis, who served as a cavalry trooper in the 8th New York Cavalry Regiment. Lewis "wore uniform & carried a sword & carbine & road & scouted & skirmished & fought like the rest" (in the words of a contemporary account). She was one of the New Afrikan soldiers who presented seventeen captured Confederate battle flags to the War Department, in a Washington ceremony. Fourteen-year-old Susie King Taylor was led out of slavery in Georgia, along with other children, by her uncle. She had already secretly learned how to read, and ended up attached to the 1st South Carolina regiment as a literacy teacher for the soldiers, nurse, and laundress. Thousands of New Afrikan women worked in Union camps, as laborers and nurses, cooks, laundresses, teachers.

Harriet Tubman might not even have been the most celebrated New Afrikan woman spy of the war. Mary Elizabeth Bowser, who worked at the Confederate White House in Richmond, secretly listened to President Jefferson Davis' strategy sessions & kept the Union informed. Under suspicion, she split with $2,500 and left the Confederate White House burning behind her. The Confederacy was riddled with New Afrikan spies, both women and men. Mary Louveste, who worked at the Confederate Navy Yard where the top-secret ironclad warship *Virginia* was under construction, took the plans to the Union Navy in Washington so they'd be ready.

Despite all the publicity around the movie *Glory*, with Denzel Washington, the Civil War has always been like white men's personal property. Their personal war, which is why so many thousands of them love to play in costume at Civil War "reenactments." But in blood-soaked real life, the stalemate that dragged on for years between Union and Confederacy was finally snapped by the New Afrikan Nation, which imposed its own agenda and forced the Confederacy to surrender.

It's true that the New Afrikan 54th Massachusetts Volunteers of *Glory* fame was special, a regiment that represented much of the New Afrikan leadership in the North. Sojourner Truth's grandson served in it, as did Martin Delany's son, and two of Frederick Douglass' sons. But thousands of New Afrikans had already taken up arms before the 54th was formed. New Afrikan militias had been formed in a number of places. Not the least of which were the Sea Islands.

Although it's seldom discussed, maritime convention and need had always let ships have multi-national and multi-lingual crews. Sailors, even white ones, were still semi-slaves at that time, without full citizenship rights and legally wards of the government. So the u.s. navy had always had many New Afrikan sailors on its ships. 30,000 New Afrikans served in the Union Navy during the war.

New Afrikan soldiers helped fight back Lee in Virginia in 1864, and led the capture of Charleston in 1865. It was known that General Sherman may have marched through Georgia, but the saying back then was "the Black regiments held open the door." The Black regiments would make up 180,000 troops, ten percent of the Union armies by the last major battles. And one-third of the standing Union Army months later at the end of 1865. These regiments were largely ex-plantation escapee forces, forming out of the substance of the South itself like an auto-immune disorder in Slavery.

And it can hardly be a surprise that they fought with a determination that struck whites on both sides.

Naturally, it was the plantation owners more quickly than anyone else who understood that New Afrikan soldiers made their downfall inevitable. Judge John Underwood of Richmond said after the war: "I had a conversation with one of the leading men in that city, and he said to me that the enlistment of Negro troops by the United States was the turning point of the rebellion; that it was the heaviest blow they ever received. He remarked that when the slaves deserted their masters, and showed a general disposition to do so and join the forces of the United States, intelligent men everywhere saw that the matter was ended."

A Multi-Faceted Reality

This should help us to come to grips with war in a deeper way. The patriarchal view of war is two-dimensional, dividing up the flowing reality into constricted boxes of macho dualities: ruler vs. subject; mind vs. body; men vs. women and children; fighting vs. building; army vs. community; military vs. political. And so on. This isn't stupidity on their part, merely a necessary construct for their kind of alienated universe. In the popular macho view, fighters are only those hitting or killing someone. Unless Harriet, for example, had put on a Union Army general's uniform and had done a book signing tour talking about how many men she had killed, she can't be recognized as a warrior. Although she saw more danger and combat than a Colin Powell or most generals and admirals, by far.

Even making a hit movie about the Black regiments only perpetuates that ideological domination. Historian Jim Cullen points out: "*Glory* obscures the ambivalence, the ambiguity, and disillusionment that military experience held for many African-American men and women during the Civil War. Indeed, the absence of Black women in the film belies their presence in many military encampments as civilians, nurses, or, in the case of Harriet Tubman, crucial strategic combatants."

Make way for liberty!

When we speak of the flow of reality, we mean, for instance, that the explosion of the New Afrikan troops was only a part of and the inevitable flowering of the mass prison breaks and over fifty years of guerrilla work in the Underground Railroad. Harriet was both a participant and one of the foremothers of the Black regiments. While they wore the Union "blue" and were under white settler officers, these soldiers were in reality a part of the New Afrikan nation and its political movement. They had a dual identity, living the possibilities of both regular soldiers of the u.s. settler empire and New Afrikan rebels against it. Unresolved for that brief moment, they wore both possibilities, one superimposed upon the other.

Even inside the u.s. military these New Afrikan soldiers took part in mass resistance against the u.s. government, against the racist policies of the Lincoln Administration. Units refused to take their pay at all, rather than accept the half of settler troops' pay that President Lincoln had ordered for them. There were protests and fights daily against colonial treatment, and even many rebellions. Eighty percent of the Union soldiers executed for mutiny during the Civil War were New Afrikans, just like in today's u.s. empire.

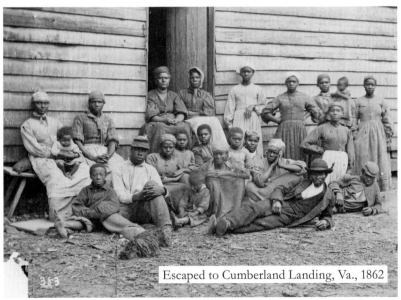

Escaped to Cumberland Landing, Va., 1862

Harriet was part of this struggle, criticizing Lincoln for his white supremacist policies. This is an important point. While Harriet is pictured today as a loyal supporter of the u.s. government and President Lincoln, in real life she never supported Abraham Lincoln until he was safely dead. Harriet, as a leader in the Anti-Slavery cause and someone who always had valuable information from behind Confederate lines, was welcome in official Washington. She had an official open invitation to visit at the Whitest House. Any time she was in Washington. Very conspicuously, Harriet refused to speak with Lincoln, whom she correctly perceived to be a crude white-supremacist.

"... I didn't like Lincoln in those days," she said later. "I used to go see Mrs. Lincoln but I never wanted to see him. You see we colored people didn't understand then that he was our friend. All we knew was that the first colored troops sent South from Massachusetts only got seven dollars a month while the white got fifteen. We didn't like that."

Harriet would drop by the Whitest House to talk politics & the conduct of the war ... but only with Ms. Lincoln. Mary Todd Lincoln is described today in history books as just another insane woman, a "shrew" who was unkind to her busy President husband. But among her contemporaries she was considered much more intellectual and radical than the President. And more sympathetic to the Black cause.

When she was in d.c., Harriet would not only meet with Mary Lincoln, but stay with u.s. secretary of state William H. Seward. Who was a supporter of Harriet's from when she was a fugitive, even though he was then a u.s senator. Harriet could tell her friends from her enemies. Although, after Lincoln was forced to sign the Emancipation Proclamation and then got assassinated, Harriet had to tactically go along & say a few nice words about him. We shouldn't be misled. Harriet was not only, in her subversive way, a player in national politics, but someone who was on the militant edge of the Black Nation's politics.

Warrior as Healer

Certainly, Harriet was respected in the Black regiments. The escaped captive William Wells Brown writes: "When the Negro put on the 'blue' 'Moses' was in her glory and traveled from camp to camp, being always treated in the most respectful manner. The Black men would have died for this woman."

Not because she was an icon, but because she was one of them & valued for what she did. Even today diseases & exposure often cause more casualties in wartime than enemy fire, and in the age before antibiotics and medivacs that was even more true.

For every white soldier who died in battle with the Union Army, two died from diseases—it was geometrically worse for New Afrikans. Due to poor health from slave life and Union racism, like being forced to do the heaviest labor and do the dirtiest jobs, living under the worst conditions. For every Black Union soldier who died in battle, ten died from diseases. In fact, one of every five New Afrikan soldiers in the Union Army ended up dying of disease. To them, a healer was as militarily essential as a skilled artilleryman or sharpshooter. Or more so.

At that time there were few useful medicines in Western medicine, and Harriet's contributions from New Afrikan healing were much in demand. Dysentery from contaminated drinking water was epidemic throughout the war in the Union camps, so often fatal. Harriet used herbal remedies New Afrikans had learned from indigenous peoples. Giving soldiers a tea she made from the powdered roots of pond lilies and parts of a flower called cranesbill, she saved many lives where settler doctors were helpless.

This shouldn't surprise our expectations. It's true that the mind of the capitalist patriarchy unnaturally divides healing from fighting, insisting that these activities be kept so separate, so isolated, that only separate persons can embody them. Like the saintly Dr. Marcus Welby, M.D. and his twin, the bloodthirsty Gen. George Patton. Yet, in the Eastern martial arts we have to learn respect for our bodies, stretching & listening to our body, as well as strikes. This is elementary. And many noted martial arts masters have been healers, and spiritual teachers as well.

During the famed Long March in 1935, Chinese communist commander Chu Teh would give basic health lectures to the guerrillas at night: About sanitation, about the simple importance of washing their feet carefully after a day's march. Is that surprising, under conditions when a blister or a dirty cut could result in crippling or fatal infection?

After arriving at Beaufort, S.C. in May 1862 on a military transport ship, Harriet reported to Gen. David Hunter, Union commander of the Department of the South. She immediately began organizing escaped New Afrikan workers in the camp, and took over the "Contraband Hospital" at Beaufort.* In a dictated letter she wrote back North:

> "Among other duties which I have, is that of looking after the hospital here for contrabands. Most of those coming from the mainland are very destitute, almost naked. I am trying to find places for those able to work, and provide for them as best as I can, so as to lighten the burden of the Government as much as possible, while at the same time they learn to respect themselves by earning their own living."

Again, Harriet was leading in *doing*, helping other New Afrikan women in practical ways to build a liberated community from

---

* In the early period of the War, escaped slaves were officially designated as "contraband." This was a legalism. Since the Lincoln Administration still recognized chattel slavery as legal, the Union had to justify not returning escaped slaves to their owners. As Rebel "property," the Army held that ex-slaves were "contraband" subject to government seizure. The name spread into common usage.

ground zero up. Her biographer writes: "She taught Negro women how to adjust to the new conditions, to produce and create articles for their own consumption ... and to make and sell various articles to the soldiers." With two hundred dollars in pay (the only government pay she would ever get, in fact) Harriet had a laundry shed built, where women could run a cooperative business doing cleaning for soldiers.

Because of the Sea Islands' importance as the first "free" territory in the Deep South, the Union had issued a general call for Abolitionists to come assist the new community. Many women, New Afrikan as well as white, came from the North to be teachers & community workers. Clara Barton, the founder of the Red Cross, came to help nurse in the hospital. To say nothing of the many formerly en-slaved "contraband" women, like the teenage Susie King Taylor, who came there.

Contrary to today's thinking, in which women say we can't do anything unless we get a grant, Harriet even gave up her few government personal privileges to better organize her people. A report to the u.s. government noted:

> "When she first went to Beaufort she was allowed to draw rations as an officer or soldier, but the freed people, becoming jealous of this privilege accorded her—she voluntarily relinquished this right and thereafter supplied her personal wants by selling pies and root beer—which she made during the evening and nights—when not engaged in important service for the Government."

No Civilians There

It's important to see that Harriet's women's organizing was only part of the many-sided flow of her life as a warrior. Isn't it true that when we hear of women & community organizing we assume without thinking that this is civilian activity, like the PTA or block improvement committee? Even our word "community" has peaceful & civilian overtones in our minds. But that wasn't it at all. Because there were no *civilians* there. And that temp community was a rear base area right in the war zone.

That "free" community that Harriet & many others were building was a small beachhead isolated far behind Confederate lines. Like a Maroon colony or a guerrilla base. While in the event of a defeat, the Union Navy might evacuate by sea the few units of Northern settler troops and settler civilians, for the many thousands of New Afrikans there would be no retreat. It was win or die.

Every person had chosen to risk their life in resistance. Whether they had hidden in the swamps & escaped through Confederate lines, or were among the thousands who had defiantly stayed behind when their so-called "owners" fled. If their community were overrun, recaptured, many would be killed and not a few like Harriet would be tortured to death. With no history, few resources, new escapees arriving daily, life was raw & chaotic in those camps. No one knew what would happen. When Harriet taught becoming self-reliant, she was preparing her sisters for survival. Even if they had to flee again & scatter. When she organized New Afrikan men & women, helped them to strengthen themselves as a people, this was life & death to them. Part of their own war. And an integral part of Harriet's life as a woman warrior.

Ironically, the laundry shed that Harriet had built for a co-operative women's enterprise was later seized by the officers of a Northern regiment, to use as their HQ. While Harriet was away on a mission to Florida. This was typical of the daily class conflicts on the Union side between settlers and New Afrikans. We have to keep in mind that this wasn't any fairy tale war of good against evil. Nor was it simply "the war to free the slaves." No way. Even as they were winning battles and dying by the thousands, many Black soldiers were completely unpaid. Since they were on wage strike & refusing to accept their apartheid pay from the u.s.government.

While in private, Lincoln & some of his generals were secretly thinking of the total elimination of the Black troops.

A Four-Sided War

The Civil War was actually a four-sided war, in which all the parties maneuvered for their own interests. In part, this was the fratricidal & incestuous "white man's war" as many described it at the time. Northern industrial capitalism and the Southern slave-owning plantation class were forced into civil war to settle which white patriarchal society would rule the continent. To both of them, New Afrikans were a factor, but only as valuable subjects for "real" people to fight over.

As we know, New Afrikans used this "falling out among thieves" to advance their own liberation. In the early months of the War, once it became clear that Northern capitalism was trying to keep New Afrikans disarmed and powerless, there was widespread sentiment among them *against* the Union war effort. Frederick Douglass spoke for many when he said that the War started: "...in the interests of slavery on both sides. The South fighting to take slavery out of the Union, and the North fighting to keep it in the Union. The South fighting to get it beyond the limits of the United States Constitution, and the North fighting for the old guarantees—both despising the Negro, both insulting the Negro."

It soon became clear that the Union would be forced, reluctant step by reluctant step, to encourage en-slaved prison breaks, to shelter escapees, to enlist New Afrikans as soldiers, and finally to end chattel slavery, to once and for all destroy the planter capitalist class and their system. Most New Afrikan activists politically united & converged on this great breakthrough, to put to death chattel slavery. Sojourner Truth put aside her pacifism to become an army recruiter; Dr. Martin Delany dropped his plan of Afrikan nationalist emigration and put on the Union "blue"; and Harriet Tubman stepped-up her guerrilla activity a thousand-fold by using the Union Army as a lever.

The fourth side to the Civil War were the indigenous nations, who were drawn into this decisive war of change. Native Amerikans took different angles to it, for both tactical & strategic reasons. Some, for example, allied with the Confederate States, under duress. But also because the first total war between white settlers & the splintering of the u.s. empire held possibilities for their own sovereignty. The Union victory was indirectly a disaster for the indigenous nations, since it resolved the major conflict holding back the westward settler aggression. The decades after the Civil War saw new "final" offensives against Native Amerikans in the West, and the birth of the attempted genocide of the reservation system.

We raise all this to stamp out lingering racist stereotypes we carry with us that the Union represented the cause of justice & that Black people reacted to the War only as enthusiastic supporters of a benevolent u.s. government.

New Afrikans as a Nation maintained their own independent politics, their critical distance. Including their own internal political debates and struggles. Not only in a need to end Southern chattel slavery, but with a healthy distrust of and need to maneuver around white settlers on both sides. Northern white society rarely saw this side because of its own white supremacy. And because New Afrikans often took over stereotypes in a transgressive way, as protective camouflage. New Afrikans on the Sea Islands, for example, tried to conceal their Gullah language & distinctive culture from the occupying Union troops.

**As early as 1861 in Virginia, escaped plantation work-
ers formed a number of outlaw guerrilla colonies, and
operated as "land pirates" preying on Confederate and
Union troops alike in an equal opportunity experiment.**
These New Afrikan guerrillas lived in hidden camps & were
aided by a supply and intelligence network of those still on
the plantations. When Gen. McClellan's Union Army of the
Potomac advanced into Virginia in 1862, so many Union
convoys were held up and white Union troops killed by New
Afrikan raiders that they had to travel heavily guarded even
behind their own lines. Keep in mind that Gen. McClellan
was the Union Army's commander-in-chief, who had not only
threatened to temporarily join the Confederates in killing any
slave revolt, but whose Union troops regularly returned escaped New Afrikans to their Confederate owners. That was the
first year of the white gentlemen's "War Between the States."

This was the difficult & conflictual war zone that Harriet
moved through. The Union Army's Department of the South
stretched along the Southeastern coast from Charleston, S.C.
to Jacksonville, Florida. In her work as an Amazon warrior
& New Afrikan general, Harriet ranged up & down the coast,
carried by Union ships. Now as a spymaster, then as a forward scout leading a raid, after that as a healer or organizer.
She flowed, with deceptive ease and without fuss, from role
to role. Any one of which might have been thought a major
achievement.

The Inevitable Resolution

In October 1862, the inevitable nodal point in change was
reached; as the growing *quantity* of New Afrikan rebellion made
a *qualitative* change in the War. Arming the New Afrikan man
had always been the wild card, the most dangerous strategic
weapon that both sides held back in reserve. Staring at defeat,

the war unpopular, the Union Army repulsed in bloody set-back after setback & even starting to shrink, the white men's government in Washington decided to form Black regiments.

As a safeguard for settler power, no more New Afrikans would become militia officers, and new units would be com-manded only by white men. This was a last resort step that even the Confederacy itself would take two years later, arm-ing thousands of its own captive New Afrikans. Hoping too late to form a "loyal" Black mercenary army of 200,000 to save it. While both sides refused to recruit women into their armies. Although over three hundred women are known to have served as regular soldiers in Union "blue" regiments. Some Confederate white women began demanding gun train-ing. Their reason wasn't to fight the Union, but to protect them-selves from the plantations' New Afrikan forced laborers while their husbands were away. And in some areas Confederate of-ficials did give pistol classes for settler women.

The white Union cavalry regiments occupying Beaufort & the Sea Islands were needed elsewhere, so the 1st and 2nd South Carolina Regiments were formed from "freed" New Afrikans. The 1st South Carolina Regiment had been formed months before Lincoln's new order, against War Department policy, and thus was the first New Afrikan unit in the u.s. army. Both regiments were commanded by white associates of John Brown and Harriet herself. One, Col. James Montgomery, had prior experience at commando warfare against the slavers, from the informal combat before the Civil War in "Bloody Kansas." During the Winter of 1862–63, the new regiments trained and started practicing their trade.

Harriet was called to organize an Intelligence Service for the Department of the South. She recruited seven New Afrikan scouts who knew the region well and were experienced at evad-ing the Southern patrols. She also recruited two New Afrikan river pilots, who were familiar with the coastal waters & riv-er systems. The ten of them made contact with networks of hundreds of anonymous New Afrikans still in chains in South Carolina, Georgia, and Florida, providing detailed information on every Confederate move. Did you think that Harriet could personally spy on hundreds of miles of enemy territory?

This fills in a picture for us. Instead of Harriet as a lone superwoman spy for a white men's army, which is what the capitalist patriarchy has wanted us to think, we can see that she was the "Commander" of a sizeable Black intelligence network. With a capital "C" as it was always put, guiding units of New Afrikan troops. Who were the spear & shield of a war zone community of embattled women, children, and men who were all liberating themselves.

Part of Harriet's work with the Black regiments then was as an intelligence officer, leading her detachment. But she also personally served as a scout, going armed with a rifle to guide the advance when the regiments struck. After the War, Gen. Rufus Saxton wrote of her: "I can bear witness to the value of her services in South Carolina and Florida. She made many a raid inside the enemy's lines displaying remarkable courage, zeal and fidelity."

Harriet herself rarely spoke of her battlefield experiences. But her grand-niece Alice Stewart remembers her & her mother visiting the elderly Harriet. The young Alice played in the tall grass of the field:

> "Suddenly I became aware of something moving toward me thru the grass. So smoothly did it glide and with so little noise. I was frightened! Then reason conquered fear and I knew it was Aunt Harriet, flat on her stomach, and with only the use of her arms and serpentine movement of her body, gliding smoothly along. Mother helped her back to her chair and they laughed. Aunt Harriet then told me that was the way she had gone by many a sentinel during the war."

After months of training, the first Black regiment was ready to fight. In January 1863, the New Afrikan troops, carried by Union gunboats, raided plantations up the St. Mary's River that divides Georgia from Florida. While that first raid brought back large quantities of rice, livestock, lumber, bricks, and iron to the hard-pressed Sea Islands, a more valuable prize soon became their target. The 2nd South Carolina Regiment was still understrength. All the intelligence reported that many still in chains there were ready to join up as soon as they saw a way to escape.

Just as the original mass jailbreak strategy of the New Afrikan nation and the experience of the Underground Railroad gave shape to John Brown's guerrilla plans, so it continued in the building raids of the Black regiments. On March 6, 1863, Gen. Saxton wrote Secretary of War Stanton about Florida, based on the reports of Harriet's Intelligence Service: "I have reliable information that there are large numbers of able-bodied Negroes in that vicinity who are watching for an opportunity to join us."

Four days later both regiments went up the St. John's River, with orders to capture Jacksonville, Florida. The ambitious Union plan was to stay and win back all of the state from the Confederacy. While the Black regiments easily seized Jacksonville, Confederate reinforcements over the next several weeks made their situation unpromising, and the regiments had to retreat back offshore. New soldiers had been recruited in Jacksonville, however, and the experience of those campaigns led to a new military strategy that Harriet herself would initiate.

Several months later the most famous episode of Harriet's life happened, when she initiated and led the Combahee River raid in June 1863. It began when Harriet told Gen. David Hunter that her plantation spies along the Combahee River in South Carolina had reported the location of all the floating mines, or "torpedoes" as they were then called, that the Confederates had placed to guard against Union attacks upriver. She felt that the rich agricultural area along the River was now ripe for invasion.

Gen. Hunter asked her, according to Harriet, "if she would go with several gunboats up the Combahee River, the object of the expedition being to take up the torpedoes placed by the rebels in the river, to destroy railroads and bridges, and to cut off supplies from the rebel troops. She said she would go if Col. Montgomery was to be appointed commander of the expedition …. Accordingly, Col. Montgomery was appointed to the command, and Harriet, with several men under her, the principal of whom was J. Plowden … accompanied the expedition."

Harriet led the raid. She wanted Col. Montgomery as the official commander because of their working relationship. Before their troops even set out, Confederate intelligence had received advance warning from agents in the North: "The *N.Y. Tribune* says that the Negro troops at Hilton Head, S.C. will soon start upon an expedition, under the command of Colonel Montgomery, differing in many respects from any heretofore projected." That was definitely a historic understatement, it turned out.

Remarkable as the night raid was, it might have been lost in history, as so many of Harriet's activities were, if it hadn't been caught in a reporter's dispatch printed in the Boston newspaper, *The Commonwealth*:

"HARRIET TUBMAN

"Col. Montgomery and his gallant band of 300 black soldiers, **under the guidance of a black woman** [emphasis in original], dashed into the enemy's country, struck a bold and effective blow, destroying millions of dollars worth of commissary stores, cotton and lordly dwellings, and striking terror into the heart of rebeldom, brought off near 800 slaves and thousands of dollars worth of property, without losing a man or receiving a scratch. It was a glorious consummation.

"After they were all fairly well disposed of in the Beaufort charge, they were addressed in strains of thrilling eloquence by their gallant deliverer ... The Colonel was followed by a speech from the black woman, **who led the raid and under whose inspiration it was originated and conducted.** For sound sense and real native eloquence, her address would do honor to any man, and it created a great sensation."

The Confederates, placing too much confidence on the river mines which Harriet quickly had disabled, were caught off guard and fled in disorder. New Afrikan soldiers advanced rapidly along both banks of the river, torching four plantations and six mills. Hundreds and hundreds of plantation prisoners reached the river, despite the plantation owners' efforts to drive them all inland. More than the three gunboats, overloaded, could carry. Harriet remembered the morning:

"I never saw such a scene. We laughed and laughed and laughed. Here you'd see a woman with a pail on her head, rice-a-smoking in it just as she'd taken it from the fire, young one hanging on behind ... One woman brought two pigs, a white one and a black one; we took them all on board; named the white pig Beauregard [a Southern general], and the black one Jeff Davis [president of the Confederacy]. Sometimes the women would come with twins hanging around their necks; it appears I never saw so many twins in my life; bags on their shoulders, baskets on their heads, and young ones tagging behind, all loaded ..."

Opposite page: **"We laughed and we laughed and we laughed,"** **Harriet would recall.** From *Harper's Weekly* July 4, 1863, illustration shows New Afrikan 2nd South Carolina Volunteers' raid on the rice plantations of the Combahee, led by Harriet Tubman the month before. Plantations can be seen burning in the distance as New Afrikan captive proletarians take advantage of the mass jailbreak.

Official Confederate Army reports admitted: "The enemy seems to have been well posted as to the character and capacity of our troops ... and to have been well guided by persons thoroughly acquainted with the river and country."

The Exact Spot of the Enemy's Imbalance

While there was a dead-on significance to the event itself, to a New Afrikan woman leading troops into action against those who believed that they had a right to "own" her people, there was also a broader impact not in Harriet as a person but in what she helped start. The use of the regiments in a New Afrikan guerrilla way, in utilizing superior intelligence to avoid confrontation & strike unexpected blows, freeing large numbers of prisoners while sinking the enemy economy, was strategic. As a warrior, she put her hand on the exact spot of her opponent's imbalance.

This was grasped by Gen. Hunter, who the next day wrote u.s. Secretary of War Stanton that the Combahee action was but an experiment of a new plan. He felt that with this approach the entire, fertile coastal areas of the Deep South, which contributed so much to the Confederate economy, would have to be completely abandoned by the Slaveocracy. All without any Northern settler reinforcements. New Afrikans would do it all themselves. Hunter immediately planned for more such raids, "injuring the enemy ... and carrying away their slaves, thus rapidly filling up the South Carolina regiments of which there are now four."

Suddenly, like a momentary clearing in a storm, we can see a brilliantly sharper picture of wars within wars. Hidden within the war of Union vs. Confederacy was always the subversive power of the New Afrikan Nation to carry out their own war. To be their own liberators. And in Harriet's life as an Amazon we see the hidden striving of millions of women as a People unto ourselves. To defy the capitalist patriarchy and to put our will upon the world.

Exhausted from several years at the front & receiving word that her aged parents needed her, Harriet took leave and went back to N.Y. in June 1864. After months of recuperation, she became involved in a new military plan. News had reached the North of a desperate Confederate effort to create a 200,000-man Black army of the South to hold back the Union. The New Afrikan mercenaries themselves would be made individually "free," of course, in return for fighting for the Slave System.

In February 1865, Confederate President Jefferson Davis told his people to recognize a bitter truth: "We are reduced to choosing whether the negroes shall fight for us or against us." Confederate soldiers sent petitions to Richmond supporting the controversial proposal, as their front lines crumbled. Finally, on February 18, 1865, General Robert E. Lee asked the Confederate Congress to authorize a Black mercenary corps: "The negroes, under proper circumstances, will make efficient soldiers." Such legislation passed at the war's end, too late to make any difference. The State of Virginia had already gone ahead and was training its first two companies of Black Confederate soldiers.

Dr. Martin Delany saw this as an opportunity. Meeting with Lincoln at the Whitest House, Delany proposed that a separate u.s. Black legion be created, officered by Black men, to prevent that Confederate threat. Delany saw this new army boldly advancing straight into the Confederate heartland: "Proclaiming freedom as they go, sustaining it and protecting it by arming the emancipated, taking them as fresh troops..."

President Lincoln, knowing that a large mercenary army fighting *for* the Confederacy could change the whole situation, surprisingly agreed to Dr. Delany's plan. Delany was tested by an army board for days & then given the rank of Major of Infantry, the first & in the Civil War the only New Afrikan to reach that rank. He was given orders to start forming his Black army in the Sea Islands. The New Afrikan strategy of the Underground Railroad, of John Brown's raid, of the Carolina regiments growing out of armed jailbreaks, reached its final form in this projected Black legion.

Of course, Delany realized just as John Brown had that the expedition needed the intelligence & propaganda services of the Underground Railroad, moving through the plantations ahead of it. His biographer writes: "Certain leading spirits of the 'Underground Railroad' were invoked. Scouts incognito were already 'on to Richmond,' and the services of the famous Harriet Tubman, having been secured to serve in the South..." Delany & Harriet, having once worked together recruiting volunteers in Canada for John Brown's guerrilla effort, again found themselves comrades in a new and even more ambitious Black military effort.

All this time, even while she had been Commander of the Intelligence Section of the Union Department of the South, Harriet had never been on the books. She was a freelance Amazon, who worked with the Union Army but who supported herself and led herself. As is our way. Not that this prevented her from making claims for money rightfully due her once the War was over. Her herstorical vision stamped its mark again after she had joined the Delany-Lincoln New Afrikan legion project.

On March 20, 1865, Harriet was in Washington to pick up her papers from the u.s. Department of War giving her passage on a transport ship from New York harbor back to the Sea Islands. A trip she never completed.

While traveling through Philadelphia on her way up to New York, Harriet was intercepted by representatives of the u.s. Sanitary Commission. They asked her help in dealing with terrible conditions in the New Afrikan hospitals run by the u.s. government near Washington, d.c. Putting a hold on her assignment, Harriet immediately traveled to the hospitals and began trying to save as many as she could. Major Delany himself had not yet sailed for the South, and wouldn't arrive there until April 3, 1865. That was the day that the triumphant Union Army captured the Confederate capital of Richmond, Virginia. Seven days later, Gen. Robert E. Lee surrendered his starving Army of Northern Virginia, and it was done.

Harriet was still more than busy, working in the hospitals for months after the War's end. In July 1865, she returned to Washington to protest the conditions in the hospitals. The result was that on July 22, 1865, u.s. surgeon-general Barnes appointed Harriet Tubman as the "matron" or woman manager of the Colored Hospital at Ft. Monroe, Virginia. Her military travel pass back there still survives. But with the end of the War her appointment never took effect, and eventually Harriet returned to Auburn, N.Y. Her parents and other family were there, and Harriet would spend the rest of her life there. Still in exile from "home," the Eastern Shore of Maryland. It was never going to be safe for Harriet to go home. She would always be a target for assassination.

It is said that Harriet "retired" after the Civil War. This is yet another misdirection. The fall of the Slave System ended an entire historical period, and began a new period where the oppressor system was based on neo-colonialism. In that new political environment Harriet was repressed out of official politics, as all New Afrikan women were. Not that she nor they ever stopped working at building the new base for the New Afrikan Nation. Or stopped publicly supporting women's struggle.

We know that Harriet is hidden in a manipulated fame, her Amazon identity dis-figured by a femmed-up image as men's supporter and helper. Even Black Nationalists have been drawn into this white tactic, paying lip service to Harriet's Amazon legacy by occasionally saying her name but really dis-missing her. We need to talk about Harriet not just as a doer of heroic deeds but as a person.

The truth is that Harriet makes amerikkkans uneasy. Because she wasn't what women are supposed to be. Yet was much more. That's why she was & is exceptionalized in such a way. Take her celebrated physical powers. Harriet's military deeds are often implicitly linked to tales of how amazingly strong she was. Not even biologically like "real" feminine women, it's silently implied. This actually has its origins right in the slaver's mouth.

Her prison-warden when she was a teenager was proud of his supposed human property. He would exhibit Harriet boastfully to his white friends. Harriet would "lift huge barrels of produce and draw a loaded stone boat like an ox." This picture is no accident. For Harriet and other New Afrikan women were only a kind of animal to euro-capitalism. Not "real" women, at all.

Some of Harriet's relatives later complained that white journalists had played up her muscular strength, making her into a freak. As we know, many New Afrikan women were physically strong. For the same reason that some six foot white u.s. marines over in 'Nam found that they couldn't carry as much as some 80-pound Vietnamese peasant grandmothers. Harriet had spent years in the fields at hard labor. Often lifting heavy weights from sunup to sundown. Plowing, handling horses, hauling logs by hand, chopping and loading heavy chunks of timber hour after hour. Developing muscles was natural in those circumstances for women as for men.

While Harriet in her youth may well have been as strong as any man on their plantation, there is no evidence of anything more. We do know that at least twice in middle age she got into scuffles with white men and, outnumbered, lost both times. The second time she was knocked unconscious. Our sis wasn't superstrong or superhuman, and she took her lumps in the rough and tumble of life. She was, however, an Amazon.

Just as a glamorous actress played Harriet on television, on several book covers she is shown as tall, muscular, and threatening. Harriet would have probably had a good laugh at that. Because, in real life, Harriet was five feet tall, slight of build, beginning to be stooped over by the time of the Civil War, missing her front teeth. She wore the cheap cotton dresses that working-class women wore then. Her one act of styling was the brightly colored bandanna that she always wore around her head. Maybe to hide the mark of her childhood injury. There is an early photograph actually showing Harriet with a group of ex-captives she has led to freedom. Harriet is hard to pick out. Short and somber, with worn face and clothes, Harriet just fades back into the band of successful escapees. So common as to be invisible.

Sometimes in science we can suddenly penetrate an ecology or culture not by what is overtly there, but by what is missing. Seeing the pattern of what is not there. While certain things about Harriet are played up, what is never discussed is Harriet's relationship to men. Both personally and in the larger sense, of her relationship to the roles for women that patriarchy made.

Harriet wasn't what women are supposed to be. Her life wasn't centered around men, she didn't swerve from her course to suit men, and she wasn't even vaguely interested in the role women were assigned. Like, Harriet never had children. Not any. Perhaps she was infertile or maybe she used birth control, but in an age when u.s. women were expected and required by the capitalist patriarchy to have six, eight, or twelve children, Harriet had none.

When she did decide to close in on a child, in 1856, she did so by just up and kidnapping her favorite niece, Margaret Stewart. On a secret visit back to Maryland, Harriet took the small child back with her without bothering to tell her brother or sister-in-law. Of course, being too busy waging war to actually raise the eight-year-old girl herself, Harriet simply dropped Margaret off with Mrs. Seward, the wife of the Governor of New York and later a u.s. senator. Sounds hard to believe, but it's a fact that Margaret grew up as an honored guest with that household. Much beloved by Harriet, Margaret nevertheless never lived with her, although they remained close all of Harriet's life. Her family said that Margaret and Harriet even looked much alike. Margaret remembered that whenever Aunt Harriet came back North, she would be sent in the Governor's horse and carriage to visit her. So much for the nuclear family.

Harriet did marry again twenty years later, in 1869, when she was about 49 years old. A young veteran in his twenties, who had met Harriet down South during the War, came to her house in Auburn, N.Y. seeking help. And Harriet took him in. That this was no romance was widely known to friends and family, and her biographer, Earl Conrad, wrote: "It has been said that her husband, Nelson Davis, spite of being a large man was not a healthy man, that he suffered with tuberculosis, and she married him to take care of him." In other words, under the family values of the times it would not have been respectable for them to live together otherwise. Davis' small pension as a Civil War veteran was the only steady income that Harriet's communal house, with its guest population of homeless children and elderly, had.

While women are supposed to be dependent, Harriet lived independent. Just like the wives of Frederick Douglass and Dr. Martin Delany, who lived working-class lives and raised their children. Anna Douglass worked as a laundrywoman and Mrs. Delany as a seamstress, to feed and clothe their children. While Frederick and Martin were often living elsewhere for years, traveling frequently, in their roles as New Afrikan leaders. But because Harriet wasn't a wife or mother, there were less obstacles to her going into combat.

Harriet Is Still Too Subversive

If men are still uneasy about Harriet, over a century later women are even more afraid to recognize her on the street. There's a continuous police action in the culture to domesticate Harriet, to rub her out as an Amazon. This continuous patriarchal theme is to erase Harriet politically. A key part of this is to whiten Harriet, to misrepresent her as being without Black feminist politics or as a "moderate." Many people have bought into this because they wanted to, even those who should know better.

Harriet's political decisions were serious decisions, and can only be understood in her situation, in its limitations and choices. i think it's exactly the radicals who don't understand their past who haven't learned to understand their own conditions, and also how to move ahead.

Women need to de-mythologize politics. There's a corrupt habit today among radicals of all kinds of demanding that the past only be a costumed fantasy to affirm our latest fashions and opinions. Of only projecting what's current back onto it. This is disingenuous, and totally harmful. One way it's corrupt is that it insinuates that politics is a verbal patriarchal power trip. Where Harriet can be politely dismissed for not talking bad enough, while men whose bold statements were only illusions that they could never make work are pointed to as positive models.

We can forget too easily how unprepared the Black Nation was; how little New Afrikan women had. They didn't have a government, although they were ruled. They didn't have schools or libraries, hospitals or churches. They had few books of their own. And a people who had not been permitted childhood naturally had nothing for children. As a people they didn't even have permanent addresses. Entire settlements were springing to life or being abandoned, in the chaotic transition out of the Slavery System. The New Afrikan community as we think of it today didn't yet exist. It had to be built. All of this had to be created for the first time, in large part by women.

Harriet stayed her course. Unlike many Anti-Slavery leaders, who took the Union victory as time to cash in their chips, Harriet lived the communal & working-class life of her people. Like many other New Afrikan women, she put her life into building the first Black institutions, the foundations of their new communities.

Development also meant self transformation, because New Afrikan women knew how unprepared they were. Almost all were illiterate. While the learned Dr. Martin Delany could write one of the first books opposing Charles Darwin and his new theory of evolution, Harriet could not read a wanted poster or a battle map. A veteran of a hundred guerrilla raids and campaigns, she once fell asleep unknowingly under her own wanted poster. Sojourner Truth, the feminist orator, was illiterate, as were her daughters. Anna Douglass, whose husband, Frederick, was the most famous Black man in amerikkka, was also illiterate. Harriet never learned to read or write, but she did throw herself into the New Afrikan literacy movement that swept the South.

There was a spontaneous mass hunger for knowing, for the power of knowledge and communication that had been denied them under Slavery. New Afrikan women could be seen outside during a work break, primary school textbook in hand trying to sound out words. Schools were set up in cabins and shacks, teaching children by day and adults at night. Harriet sent all the funds she could raise (and much of her personal earnings) to help support two of the new community schools.

For years, as Harriet would lead her fellow fugitives through the North, on the way to Canada and temporary safety, she would use the first African Methodist Episcopal churches as shelters. Where the band of escaped fugitives could hide among sisters & brothers, rest and be fed. These few churches were the only centers an oppressed people in a hostile land had. Deeply moral, Harriet joined with other New Afrikan women in the area to conduct revival meetings, to start new churches wherever they could. Her own house in Auburn, N.Y. she turned into a communal resource. She put up children whose parents could not afford to support them, elderly Anti-Slavery movement veterans and guests. She wanted to set up a self-supporting farm, which would operate the "John Brown Home" as she called it. As a resource for the community. She lived her life constructing the grassroots of the Nation, upon which the Ida B. Wellses and countless other women of later generations would stand.

Victory and defeat change everything. Harriet Tubman was the product of an en-slaved communal nation. That's why she was so military. Her movements were more natural because she was never subordinate within her people. Harriet could work in the Underground Railroad *with* men and not be a subordinate.

The death of Moses was a signal event. An Amazon that Slavery and armed white men had not been able to stop. But Harriet could no longer be the General, could no longer be Moses. Again, this isn't just about one Amazon. Here in modern history, not thousands of years ago before recorded time, we can see in detail how the development of patriarchal classes changed the nature of women and men in war. This is a modern change, that can be remade or reversed in our lifetime. This is the subject here.

Harriet is still too subversive, still really hard to deal with. One reason even radicals fall into the trap of treating her non-politically. Dis-missing her as a simple minded woman. They don't say it, but they mean it. What's so hard to swallow is that her deeds didn't come from super abilities, like an Einstein, but from qualities that we're all supposed to have. And that, em-barrassingly, most of us have only momentary glimpses of.

More than anything else, Harriet was deeply rooted. In herself as an Amazon and in her New Afrikan people. **And being so centered, there was a deceptive fluidity to everything she did. For her there was no distance between "I should" and "I did." She simply lived her politics to the fullest.**

If Harriet wasn't what women are supposed to be, even more threatening was that she was much more. Not only independent of men, but a player in their closely monopolized territory of war and politics. Harriet was out of men's control, but as a New Afrikan woman was also considered by white men to be lowly and unimportant. An attitude Harriet took big time advantage of. In fact, had she tried to join or reform the patriarchy she never would have gotten anything done. Harriet took guerrilla advantage of her informal, unorthodox status to slip beneath the radar of men's restrictions. After all, as "Private Harriet" or "Corporal Harriet" she never would have been able to confer with Union leaders and generals, or guide their decisions by shaping their Intelligence.

We need to go back to something we said earlier: Once out of Slavery, Harriet never put herself under the command of men. Make no mistake, Harriet understood hierarchy & patriarchy quite well. Literally under the lash for 29 years, bearing whip scars she would carry all her life, working with fugitive slaves and Union commanders alike, she had a very practical grasp of men's hierarchy. But she never followed it.

Harriet worked with male leaders of the Anti-Slavery movement, not under them. Just as she worked with the Union Army, but reserved the right to do whatever she felt best at any time. She wasn't confined by a career or a rank in the hierarchy. And you know she wouldn't have been able to fight a war if she had to be home for dinner.

Harriet rode the waves of her People's struggle, and became a leader. Their victories and losses, their choices right & wrong, were the preconditions for the Malcolm Xs and Audre Lordes that came later. Harriet didn't have to always win, or save her People single-handed. What's crucial is that as an Amazon, Harriet took her turn at bat. She made political choices. She did what she had to do to fight out the great issues of the day.

Guerrilla, farmhand, lumberjack, laundress and cook, refugee organizer, raid leader and Intelligence commander, nurse and healer, revival speaker, feminist and fundraiser. Harriet flowed, without fuss, from need to need, task to task. Having no power, she could live with immeasureable power. That's what makes her such a difficult model. You can't get a grant to be Harriet. And while the capitalist patriarchy has a million schools, women still do not have even one school to teach what Harriet could do.

In her old age a newspaper reporter from the *N.Y. Herald* came to interview her, one of the last surviving heroines of the Anti-Slavery struggle:

> "She looked musingly toward a nearby orchard, and she asked suddenly: 'Do you like apples?' On being assured I did, she said: 'Did you ever plant any apple trees?' With shame I confessed that I had not. 'No,' said she, 'but somebody else planted them. I liked apples when I was young, and I said: "Some day I'll plant apples myself for other young folks to eat," and I guess I did.'"

(not the end)

"THE EVIL OF FEMALE LOAFERISM"

"THE EVIL OF FEMALE LOAFERISM"

HARRIET TUBMAN AS A GUERRILLA existing beyond the leadership of men, proved how even one Amazon with the right leverage can bend the world to her will. But Harriet herself was hardly a lone superwoman. In fact, that's the sharp point here. Her generation of the en-slaved Nation was the product of centuries of underground prison learning, development of their own imperfect communalism, and her-oic resistance at great cost. They finally broke out in a revolution that trashed and then overthrew the actually-existing capitalism of their time & place. That's what the chattel slavery system was.

The most important thing here to understand is that women are players amidst many forces shaping and reshaping the world. We aren't just the damn fixtures in the men's room.

The risings of New Afrikan women in Harriet's lifetime and beyond are pictures of this truth. However unorthodox and always surprising by the standards of men's his-story. No matter how often it is suppressed and papered over in this culture of false memory. Mainstream euro-capitalism wants everyone to only stare fixedly at a Hollywood movie-like story of the u.s. Civil War. With its white settler men in blue uniforms and the white settler men in grey uniforms wrestling in the mud and slaughtering each other, the main show in the main arena. Not the truth, just more patriarchal capitalist propaganda that's only "real" like sleek automobile ads on television are "real."

What's true is that then as now there were wars within wars, a mixed solar system of classes and combatants in which women of the varied nations and peoples and races were players. Often placing their intentions and weight on the shape of the conflicts. No one was staying home to redecorate the dining room, you can be sure of that.

For instance, herstorian and Harvard University president Drew Gilpin Faust, has often suggested that perhaps the subversion of Southern white women themselves determined the 1865 collapse of the Confederacy. By the time General Robert E. Lee was forced to surrender his rebel army to Union General Ulysses S. Grant, over 80% of the soldiers carried on his official rolls had long since deserted. Many in response to insistent letters from home, from their wives and mothers. Confederate General Joseph E. Johnson wrote: "It was not uncommon for a soldier to be written to by his wife ... that it was necessary that he should return home to save them from suffering or starvation ... Such a summons, it may well be supposed, was never unheeded ... increasing the likelihood of military defeat."

The plans of Confederate President Jefferson Davis and his war cabinet to reinforce the supplies of their hungry armies, were directly sabotaged by the many Confederate women who started staging "bread riots" to feed their families. Directly refusing the "everything for our soldiers" dictates of the Confederacy's male leaders and the wealthy food merchants they were allied to. Spontaneous crowds of white women evolved militarily into women's gangs that agreed to simply seize what they needed by force. As in the early "bread riot" in the Confederate capital of Richmond, Virginia, in April 1863. The women who had agreed to fight together in Richmond, came back to the stores and state warehouses the next day after arming themselves with pistols, large knives, hammers, and hatchets. Those newly come without weapons, often took up stones and sticks right then and there. To fight their way into the government food stores.

That Richmond, Virginia action was largely made up of working-class white women, many who worked at the large iron works making artillery or were the wives of Confederate civil servants. One of the main speakers at their first rally was 34-year-old Mary Jackson, who was normally self-supporting buying and selling veal at a market. The several hundred armed women protested at the governor's mansion. They

Engraving from *Frank Leslie's Illustrated Newspaper*, (1863 May 23). Entitled "Sowing and Reaping" the captions read "Before and after pictures of 'Southern women hounding their men on to rebellion' and '...feeling the effects of rebellion and creating bread riots'."

broke into depots and stores, finding and taking hams and tins of butter, bags of scarce salt for preserving, and bags of flour. This was the largest civil disturbance within settler ranks in the history of the Confederacy. Eventually with thousands of women and even men, which amounted to an estimated ten percent of the capital's entire population, either taking some part or as cheering bystanders.

The Confederate ruling class vacillated, unsure whether to repress or try to censor news of these outrageous white women. In Richmond, artillery units were deployed outside the government headquarters, and white women were warned that they would be fired on in any future attempts. Mary Jackson herself was denounced afterwards in cute language by the *Richmond Sentinel* newspaper as an "Amazonian huckster," while the other women were called "professional thieves, prostitutes and gallows birds of every hue & nationality." Such white women's illegal direct actions spread to Greenville, Greensboro, Petersburg, Columbus, Mobile, and beyond.

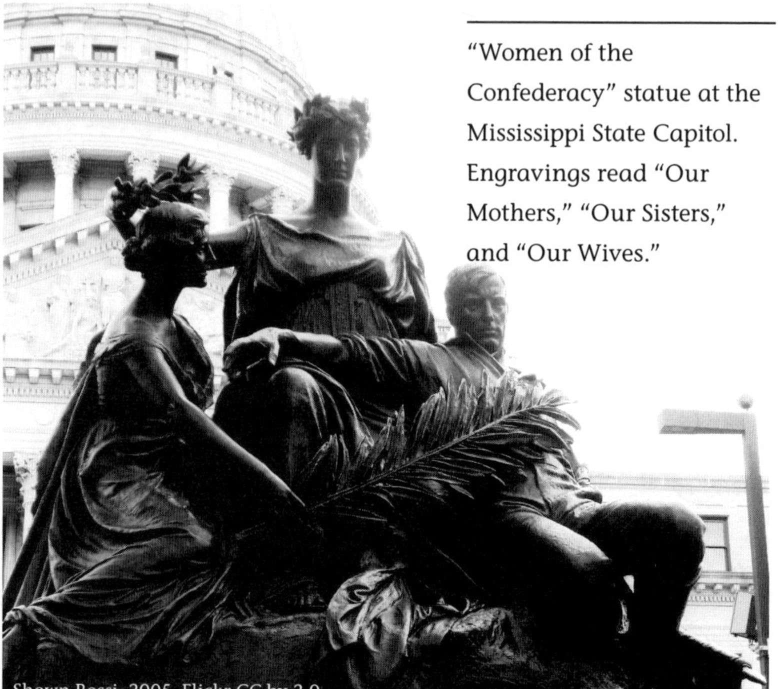
Shawn Rossi, 2005. Flickr CC by 2.0.

"Women of the Confederacy" statue at the Mississippi State Capitol. Engravings read "Our Mothers," "Our Sisters," and "Our Wives."

In Mobile, the settler women passed out leaflets and carried banners with a slogan taken from the French Revolution of 1789: "Bread or Blood." They drove off paramilitary units of males sent to stop them. Soon enough, the Confederate state and the local governments were forced to open warehouses and start programs of food relief. In a mass diversion of supplies originally meant to be divided between the weakening army and the wealthy.

Though the women's "bread riots" throughout the Confederacy never completely stopped. As late as February 1865, the Macon, Georgia journal *The Southern Confederacy* reported: "A disgraceful affair is now going on up town. A mob of women with a black flag, are marching from store to store on a pillaging expedition ..."

It isn't true that settler women in the South then had no politics, and were simply passively obeying whatever men did. They decided to intervene and get in the capitalist patriarchy's way in order to take care of their own interests, even if it meant the downfall of the whole damn Confederacy. And it certainly was a part of that fall.

But in the same light, they then promptly went back to ardently supporting violent settler colonial rule over New Afrikan captives in their new, more complex postwar world. This is a very important point. It foreshadowed what even more white women were to do after the Women's Suffrage movement at the turn of the 20th century and then do again after the 1960s Women's Liberation movement. Always going back to settler men and the capitalist patriarchy. This isn't true of New Afrikan women, who have never reconciled to the rule of white men to this day.

All their politics were real, were conscious, were choices they had made. And what was true for those white women, was even more true for New Afrikan women newly "risen" from chattel slavery.

Because we know so little, we have to go back to pick up the threads of the pattern. Way back long before Obama and Ferguson, before Bush and Katrina, before Civil Rights. When the struggle was more raw, more visible. To learn pattern recognition from that her-story so that we can use it in our present moment.

Women as a gender-class are always hidden in his-story. By definition. Hidden so that we *don't* learn as we should from struggles like the class war of the u.s. ruling class versus New Afrikan women as a gender-class. The cutting edge of a Black Nation. A struggle that only became sharper, more visible, *after* the Civil War and *after* the fall of chattel slavery.

New Afrikan women were leading in new resistance struggles; this most radical resistance from the New Afrikan Nation is largely undiscussed now, because it was coming from a different direction. It was a mass breakout led by women away from coercive capitalism as they had known it. Having little to do with men's politics and directly bucking men's governments. We are talking about witnessing an example of women's war with capitalism.

This is something that slides by us; that is hidden and that we don't study. **Unlike white men, who study the mechanics and strategies of all their battles. Including labor struggles. We need to study how New Afrikan women took the offensive. To learn how wars and battles were done. So we can do them ourselves. Amazons need to study this as a practical thing, not to put up some memorial or just to say how great Black women are.** As a revolutionary practice we need to know how independent women fought back. And started stepping off from capitalism, founding rear base areas. We need to know the strengths and weaknesses of new ways of doing things.

Richmond in ruins

The Permanent Women's Strike
That Changed the u.s. Empire

As soon as the Civil War was on, New Afrikans in the Slave South naturally took advantage of it by increasing resistance. Slowdowns in the fields, sabotage, strikes, breakdowns in production, mass escapes to the Union lines, became common. As early as 1862, when Union forces recaptured New Orleans and nearby parts of Southern Louisiana, captive New Afrikan women started leading strikes on the plantations there demanding cash wages. For almost three centuries on that land New Afrikans had been without human rights much less a payday. Early in the War, remember, the Whitest House and Congress still wanted to hold the door open to chattel-slavery in some form. Which was still upheld by the law of the land. In many instances at the start of the Civil War, Union army units would return escaped New Afrikans back to Slavery. To force the planter-capitalists to give up wages was not a small thing to a people who were counted as property. After all, you don't pay wages to property. You force its submission.

For that generation of New Afrikan women, that was a time of leading monumental changes for their people on a scale seldom seen by any of us. We tell this her-story to honor their towering memory—for which there are no monuments in any of men's capitals. And that their will and genius will lend strength to women everywhere on this battleground.

Naturally, this rising swallowed up the entire South after the collapse of the Confederacy in 1865. *And grew more radical and more woman-centered.* This was a crisis for the u.s. ruling class, which had intended to continue the massive exploitation of Black workers only with Wall Street on the top as the big bosses. The agricultural exports produced by New Afrikan labor in the South, the sugar and rice and tobacco and especially amerikkka's biggest cash export commodity, "King Cotton," were essential to the whole u.s. economy.

Many New Afrikan women throughout the South literally disappeared from the plantation labor force, in what became the greatest labor strike in the history of the u.s. empire. Enslaved women, who had been the targets of close, hateful, often sadistic supervision by overseers and capitalists, wanted nothing more than to separate themselves from euro-settlers. Reacting to the fall of the Confederacy by moving to physically separate themselves and their children from white people and the plantation as much as possible. **The power of the deliberate separatism argued for a century later by radical nationalists such as Malcolm X, was earlier seen in practice in this movement of New Afrikan women.** This was a People's strategy which swept the South as a mass movement.

Single New Afrikan women with children often tried leaving the rural areas altogether, particularly since feeding children ceased to be desirable to the plantation owners once they could no longer sell them on the slave auction block. The urban New Afrikan population of the South grew by 75% right after the Civil War, and was heavily woman-centered. One study reports: **"In 1870 the ratio in both Atlanta and Wilmington, North Carolina, was about four to three [Black women to men]. In New Orleans the number of Black women aged fifteen to forty-five exceeded that of men in the same age bracket by more than fifty percent."** The New Afrikan city within a white city was at this critical period a *women's* city.

Women began to withdraw completely from the old plantations. Which were not scenic "farms" as white nostalgia likes to pretend, but brutal, large-scale agricultural factories built on life-long prison labor. Shielding their own children from growing up in prison-like conditions under meddlesome settler supervision was a priority. So they tended their own vegetable gardens, fished and gathered, traded among themselves, did laundry and other part-time cash labor. They both physically left the plantations and boycotted any reappearance of the old labor gangs. This mass strike eventually led to the downfall and end of many historic plantations as ongoing businesses. To be replaced by the dividing up of the land for sharecropping & tenant farming, a still exploitative but more indirect form of labor oppression. Not only did women fight for separate farmland of their own, but within families often the year-round labor for the white plantations was left to the men.

After the disappointing cotton harvest of 1867–68, a report by Boston cotton brokers blamed the trend of *"growing numbers of Negro women to devote their time to their homes and children."* There was widespread support from New Afrikan men for this women's labor boycott. A Yankee cotton buying agent reported: *"One thing the people are universally opposed to. They all swear they will not work in a gang ..."* One of the men's favorite arguments with white planters and government officials was that since white women were supposed to concern themselves with childraising and the home, no one should complain if Black women did the same. Flipping patriarchal stereotypes back against the capitalist with a straight face.

Government officials concerned with the South made no secret that New Afrikan women had a special obligation to serve u.s. business by laboring in the fields. U.S. Freedmen's Bureau agent John DeForest in South Carolina wrote in a perfect sexist snit about how *"myriads of women, who once earned their own living, now have aspirations to be like white ladies and, instead of using the hoe, pass the days in dawdling over their trivial housework, or gossiping among their neighbors."* Any women's freedom at all really got under the skin of white men.

At the extreme of economic resistance, some New Afrikan women and men resisted recapture back into the patriarchal capitalist economy's agricultural proletariat so long as they had free access to nature. One example was recorded in the letters of euro-settler plantation owner Frances Leigh, who returned to the Sea Islands off South Carolina in 1865 to take back her family's plantation. Leigh confidently expected that hunger would force her family's former prisoners back to the

The u.s. Freedmen's Bureau was set up in 1865, as the very first Federal government social work and welfare agency. In an age before white men had learned to watch their tongues, it was designated as a combination relief charity, nanny and supervisor at large specifically for Black people. And, of course, to try and force important capitalist cultural values such as male supremacy & loyalty to empire into their heads. A creature of the Union military occupation of the defeated South, the Bureau set up small regional offices usually staffed by a former white army officer. These agents had great power over the former enslaved workers. Each functioned as a welfare provider, a judge in their one-man court to settle problems with New Afrikans, and as nosy social workers. Temporary food rations were given out at first to close to a million New Afrikans (one out of every four alive then), while many crude one-room schoolhouses and even a few hospitals were set up. The Bureau was abolished as unnecessary by Congress in 1872, but its example has lived on in the patriarchal capitalist state to this day.

cotton fields. Soon, however, she was writing with bitterness: *"...it is a well-known fact that you can't starve a negro."* While many were forced to return on the plantation owners' terms, others nearby refused to do wage labor at all but survived with *"no difference whatever in their condition"* without wages as far as plantation owner Leigh could see. By fishing, growing vegetables, gathering, trapping, and trading services. Not being crazy, New Afrikans fresh out of Slavery were taking a break from capitalism any way they could.

Just having broken out of imprisonment, New Afrikan women were not so dazed as many white his-torians have insinuated. From the start, New Afrikan women throughout the South were fighting for farmland of their own. To be the farmers, the people in charge themselves. To be materially independent of men, as free people. Her-storian Paula Giddings reminds us that activist Frances Ellen Harper, in her reports while traveling through the South, *"wrote of numerous women who successfully worked farms alone or with another woman as partner. 'Mrs. Jane Brown and Mrs. Halsey formed a partnership ten years ago,' Harper reported in 1878. The women 'leased nine acres and a horse. And cultivated the land all that time, just as men would have done. They saved considerable money from year to year, and are living independently' ... "*

Escaping slave convoy takes everything they can.

Partial Separation A First Step

Just as escaping from bondage before the Civil War was far more than just "running away," separating from the plantation regimentation of daily life was much more than just "wanting a better job." To return to that earlier example: those mass slave escapes had created a *rear base area* in the North and Canada. A breathing space where New Afrikan communities could grow & educate themselves. Build schools of their own & churches, and prepare themselves as a people for the storm of the ongoing war. From this rear base area in the North grew not only the structure of the "Underground Railroad" but the later volunteers of the Black Regiments. Not only guerrillas and regular infantry but political leaders raising different strategies and choices. Not only Frederick Douglass and Martin Delany, but Harriet Tubman and Sojourner Truth.

This concept of rear base areas, a major part of guerrilla strategy, is invaluable here to us. Because the outward forms of women's struggles are often different from men's, we need to keep these underlying strategic concepts in mind. Just to bring what women have done & can do out from the shadows of patriarchy.

In guerrilla strategy, rear base areas are one of the essential elements for successful war. They are a space that is temporarily less contested, away from the main strength of the enemy. Where the resistance can build itself. Often protected by distance and borders of one kind or another, whether mountain ranges or different states or cultural structures. In these temporarily more sheltered spaces guerrillas rest & build. They train, start new formations and strategies. This connects especially to a second major communist guerrilla concept — that of the *strategic defensive*, as Mao called it. Macho or macha warfare seeks to attack the enemy as soon as possible, to trade blows in decisive battles. While guerrilla strategy seeks the opposite in its first stage. To avoid anything decisive. To retreat away from the heavier blows of the more powerful oppressor. Quietly "trading space for time" in order to gradually become a new kind of power.

The need for women to always find new spaces in men's world relates in strategy to this. Whether the temporarily freer space to build in is physical or cultural—or both. So women's refusal to rejoin plantation labor gangs under white overseers—their move to boycott plantations altogether—was a struggle to create a kind of rear base area. Where they could not only have a freer life on a daily basis, but find the time & terrain to become a different people. Not unimportant as a strategy for an oppressed people.

This became one battle in the ongoing struggle that still rages today over who will control New Afrikan women's bodies. As with all women's bodies.

Because women are the production site of human reproduction, our bodies have always been the most important property in men's class societies. "Your body is a battleground" is one of the truths that the liberation of women teaches. Even in the cosmopolitan, affluent, post-industrial cities of today's patriarchal capitalism, the battles rage away with no end in sight. Not just over whether men or women will control our bodies, but even over *which* of the clashing groups of men will own us.

Reproduction was revealed then in its true light in patriarchal capitalism, as a basic economic activity. Entire *communities* of captive Afrikan women throughout the Western Hemisphere often fought back using their partial control over reproduction. The use of natural abortifacients was common in Black colony after Black colony. Along the East Coast, New Afrikan women used wild tansy to interrupt pregnancy. The leaves and stalks of the cotton plant itself in the Deep South were also chewed as a mild abortifacient. It is hard to know exactly how effective these were, since they blended into the harsh conditions, the overall miscarriage rate for pregnant New Afrikan women in the Slave South often being fifty percent or higher.

We can understand, then, how fiercely the battle over women's bodies raged during the Slavery System and after. Because to the slaveowner capitalist, the reproduction and selling of new slaves was an economic activity as profitable as the raising of the cotton itself. Young captive women were reminded that bearing children would help persuade the capitalist not to "sell them South." Former u.s. president Thomas Jefferson highly valued New Afrikan women. Because they supported his parasitic lifestyle, sipping French wines in a splendid pseudo-Grecian mansion. As he proudly admitted: *"I consider the labor of a breeding woman no object, and that a child raised every two years is of more profit than the crop of the best laboring man."* That was a "great" u.s. president speaking, the man who personally wrote the u.s. Declaration of Independence.

After the fall of the Confederacy, New Afrikan women were quick to fight for the right to not use their bodies for reproduction except as they chose. Just as they fought for their right to turn their energy towards raising children who would grow up to be free. As Rose Williams, who had been forced to live with a man she disliked, swore: "... I's never wants no truck with any man. De Lawd forgive dis cullud woman, but he have to 'scuse me and look for some others for to 'plenish de earth."

Childbearing rates went down steadily. By the early 1900s one out of four New Afrikan women had no children, and fully one-half of all New Afrikan married women with some education had no children at all. Much higher rates of non-childbearing than with white women.

Opposite page: Sorting cotton, Sea Islands, from *Frank Leslie's Illustrated Newspaper*, 1869.

Wars Within Wars Fought on the Same Ground

This massive class stand by women resisting re-enslavement caused alarm bells to go off from Wall Street to New Orleans. Yankee businessmen and Southern plantation owners alike united around their need to end "the evil of female loafer-ism," as South Carolina u.s. Freedmen's Bureau agent John DeForest thundered with totally unconscious humor. In Georgia, one plantation owner complained: "One third of the hands are women who now don't work at all."

There were *multiple* wars going on way back then, being fought on the same territory and time, not *one*. This overlay of one war on top of another with a different grain confused many after the Civil War, and still confuses many today. This confusion is deliberate by "post-civil rights" patriarchal capitalism.

The most obvious war was the u.s. Civil War. The huge spectacle of two clashing uniformed armies of euro-amerikkkan settlers both commanded by West Point graduates. Representing Northern industrial capitalism versus Southern slave labor agricultural capitalism, two conflicting variants of capitalist cultures and hierarchies. Like two brother mafias "going to the mattress" as in *The Godfather,* to determine which will own all the crime. That most advertised war, from 1861–1865, was the bloodiest and most costly u.s. war ever, by far. It ended with chattel slavery being banned and the former plantation capitalist class that had owned it bankrupted and defeated.

We have to call timeout for a second. Some new readers will unthinkingly go along with the seductive flow of u.s. patriarchal capitalist mis-history around the toilet bowl. i call it "mis-history" to underline its deliberate fictional quality, though all men's history is a lie in the first place. It is widely believed, as patriarchal capitalism intends, that in the u.s. empire all slavery was ended with the ending of one specific chattel slavery after 1865. Not so, sister.

u.s. capitalism was desperate to somehow contain this subversive New Afrikan women's strike throughout the defeated Confederacy. "Female loaferism" was not a laughing matter to patriarchal capitalism, which could not even pretend to be profitable without its coerced workers. And, of course, that women's labor rebellion ran alongside all the other militant actions of the self-liberated New Afrikan proletariat after 1865: the organization into Black unions and associations of all types as well as openly armed militias, with walkouts and direct takeovers of territory and crops. The capitalist state counter-attacked right away with two big weapons: criminalization and cooptation. From this counter-attack came a reforging of New Afrikan slavery but in the legalized garment of convict labor and segregation throughout the South.

We always have to remember that it is the male ruling class of every epoch who defines what is "criminal" and what is not for everyone. Often the same action is perfectly legal for one generation of workers or oppressed but severely punished for the next. The feudal tenants in Old Europe often had the traditional right of gathering fallen branches for firewood in the lord's forests, along with ground-nuts and other non-crops from the underbrush. But when capitalism commercialized their relationship, the same gathering by peasants of "nature's bounty" was criminalized as "theft" or a kind of "poaching." This was exactly what happened to New Afrikan women after the Civil War.

The first counter-move was to block New Afrikan women from directly sustaining themselves by Nature or from the products of their own people's labor.

That was done first through the infamous Black Codes, which the immediate post-war Southern state governments passed to replace the bullet-riddled Slave Codes. Those discarded codes had legally dis-ordered New Afrikan life under the old Slavery System for over a century.

For example, en-slaved New Afrikan prisoners on the plantations had often been underfed to the point of starvation for the hard labor they did. **Although it was completely illegal under actually-existing capitalist law, New Afrikans as a whole assumed a "natural right" to appropriate any food they could to sustain themselves and particularly their children.** While a few women hunted late at night for small game in the woods, "hunting" at night for pieces of meat from the plantation smokehouse or eggs from the chicken coop, or taking bit by bit some of the plantation's crop for underground sale was commonplace. "Necessity knows no law." It became like part of an ever-present social background, and not by itself a big deal to either side at the time.

So after the Confederacy's downfall, New Afrikan women and their families savored the freedom previously denied them of staying as far away as possible from settler capitalists. While at the same time insisting on a "moral economy" in which they had a right to share in whatever of society's they needed to survive.

One herstorian says of this people's economy right after the Civil War: "Tending a garden was not the only means by which black family members sought to keep themselves fed during these turbulent times. Although some freedpeople spirited rice from baskets and cotton from bins (to be disposed of on local black markets), most stalked livestock or raided smokehouses to stave off starvation. Indeed, blacks often perceived their ill-gotten gain as 'a supposed right' not only in a response to a system that exploited their labor in a most calculated way, but also in response to individual planters who reneged on their agreement, expressed or implied, to furnish freed families throughout the year."

The planter capitalists themselves reneging on the annual contractual promise of food for their workers' families in the "slack season" was one root cause of conflict. In a typical report, u.s. Freedmen's Bureau Agent J.A. Yordy reported from Eutaw, Alabama in May 1868, after such unpunished violations by local white planters: "Shoats and Poultry seem to be mainly in quest, and they are disappearing beyond precedent…" Since New Afrikans out of necessity, he wrote, "Supply their families as best they can, this compels them to divide their Scanty rations with their families or resort to Stealing as the only alternative." One class's crime is only another class's justice.

Our herstorian further sums up:

"Predictably, employers complained bitterly about the efforts of blacks to provide for themselves; the authorities in Marksville, Louisiana, went so far as to arrest a black woman and three of her kinfolk for venturing 'into a field and picking from the ground a few walnuts.' The privileges or 'customary rights' accorded some antebellum slaves evolved into prerogatives that freedpeople jealously guarded at their own peril. Women took time from the fields to sew for their friends and families, to dry fruit, and to tend pigs and chickens. Husbands and sons made furniture and baskets to use at home or sell in the marketplace; chopped wood, always in demand by riverboats and mills; and trapped animals and fished in order to supplement the household's diet.

"As a matter of law, foraging permitted by slaveowners became unacceptable to postwar employers. Under South Carolina's Black Codes, for example, blacks who hunted or fished could be prosecuted as trespassers or vagrants. During the 1860s and 1870s throughout the Black Belt, planters pressed for new legislation that would restrict access of blacks (and landless whites) to forests and streams and thus curtail opportunities for foodstuff self-sufficiency."

The Black Codes or the state laws specifically regulating New Afrikan behavior, were the legal form by which Afrikan slavery was reborn after the Civil War into a new system of criminalization. In a way which resonates still into our own 21st century present. It was the very post-1865 reforms to the u.s. Constitution which permitted and recast this New Afrikan "involuntary servitude." *It shouldn't surprise anyone that it has been revolutionary prisoners who have led in pointing this out.* In 1971, writing from her cell in the Marin County jail in California awaiting trial for armed rebellion, Angela Davis reminded us of those Black Codes and re-enslavement—and the illegal struggle which was rekindled as well. She wrote: "Even as slavery faded away into a more subtle yet equally pernicious apparatus to dominate black people, 'illegal' resistance was still on the agenda. After the Civil War, Black Codes, successors to the old Slave Codes, legalized convict labor ... and generally codified racism and terror."

Only a few years later, the New Afrikan Prisoners Organization writing in 1977 from Stateville Prison in Illinois, reminded everyone that the passage of the u.s. 13th Amendment to the Constitution was the "Instrument of Legalized Slavery and the Re-Subjugation of New Afrika":

> "While these words are being written, a U.S. Prisoners'
> Petition to the United Nations is being circulated
> throughout amerikkka, both inside and outside prison
> walls. The Petition, which is to be presented to the U.N.
> Subcommission on the Prevention of Discrimination and
> the Protection of Minorities between August 22nd and
> September 9, 1977, in Geneva, Switzerland, states in part:
> 'AS PRISONERS WE PROTEST: The subjugation of all prisoners to involuntary servitude and slavery. The 13th amendment to the u.s. constitution states, *"Neither slavery, nor involuntary servitude, except as a punishment for crimes where the party shall have been duly convicted, shall exist within the united states, or any place subject to their jurisdiction."'*

> "We protest the 13th amendment which legalizes slavery
> in the u.s. Our protest and condemnation of the practice
> of slavery is upheld by international United Nations law,

which states: 'No one shall be held in slavery or servitude; slavery or the slave trade shall be prohibited in all their forms.'"

The New Afrikan Prisoners Organization pointedly added: "It was never the intention of the rulers of the u.s. to 'abolish' slavery. That is, it was never their intention to discontinue the domination and exploitation of Afrikan people in the u.s."

Because of that constitutional loophole through which the Black Codes were slipped by Southern governments, we could see tragic sights like the one captured in an old black & white engraving in the journal, *Frank Leslie's Illustrated Newspaper,* January 19, 1867. In which a young New Afrikan man stands respectably dressed in suit and tie, his hat in hands, before the crowd in front of a courthouse—being auctioned off. The caption reads: "Selling a Freedman to Pay His Fine at Monticello, Florida."

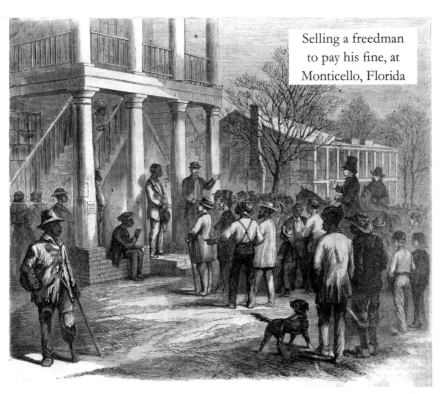

Selling a freedman to pay his fine, at Monticello, Florida

The Black Codes illegalized "female loaferism" or any New Afrikan escape from capitalist labor. Throughout the South, laws applying only to New Afrikans were passed which made "vagrancy" and "disrespect" crimes. Not being employed in the settler economy, quitting or even being absent from a job without permission, talking back to a settler, not laboring hard enough to suit settler employers, all became crimes. And crimes which led to being on the modern auction block, with months or even years of forced labor ahead of you after some settler company or plantation or employer purchased your lease.

The demand for such cheap captive labor was so great that extra New Afrikan crimes were created out of thin air, such as having a disorderly family, not dressing well enough, idling in public, making insulting gestures to settlers, being careless with money, and drinking too much. Then there were crimes of resistance, such as having a firearm or refusing to literally bow to settler women as a sign of submission. Nor were children in any way exempted. In one well-known case in Mississippi, where one of every four convict laborers were said to be children, six-year-old Mary Gay was sentenced to thirty days, and a fine for "court costs" which would have to be worked off also. For that six-year-old girl-child allegedly trying to take a hat.

As Angela Davis wrote, the hypocrisy of how the u.s. 13th amendment and the Black Codes "simultaneously acknowledged and nullified black people's new juridical status as U.S. citizens":

> "The racialization of specific crimes meant that, according to state law, there were crimes for which only black persons could be 'duly convicted'. The Mississippi Black Codes, for example, which were adopted soon after the close of the Civil War, declared vagrant 'anyone who was guilty of theft, had run away [from a job, apparently], was drunk, was wanton in conduct or speech, had neglected job or family, handled money carelessly, and ...

all other idle and disorderly persons.' Thus vagrancy was coded as a black crime, one punishable by incarceration and forced labor."

After having his legislation outlawing chain gangs, segregated transportation, and voting restrictions thrown out by new settler majorities elected through terrorism, Georgia state legislator Aaron Bradley went to Washington in May 1870. Testifying futilely before Congress, Bradley shouted to deaf ears:

> "Little girls and boys under ten years of age are sent to chain-gangs for three potatoes or singing Shoo-fly, with great locks and chains around their necks; colored bogusly-convicted women and men are let out for ten cents a day to do out-door work that should be done by honorable white and colored laborers at $1.50 per day, and never permitted to vote after it. Any colored person can be convicted for anything, and white men cannot be convicted for anything done to negroes."

Convict labor has always been marginalized as an issue, dismissed as a brutal but minor part of the general backwardness of the post-Confederate South. Not only was criminalization and the resulting "involuntary servitude" a calculated act of state terrorism to break "female loaferism" specifically and New Afrikan resistance as a whole, but it virtually founded the modern gulag system in those states. As James Yaki Sayles, speaking for the black liberation army-coordinating committee, always pointed out: before the overthrow of chattel slavery amerikkka basically didn't need prisons. Almost all New Afrikans were already imprisoned labor on the plantations, while most crimes by white men were perfectly legal.

To take Georgia as an example: before the end of chattel Afrikan slavery there hardly was a separate "prison system." For colonialism, subjugation *was* the prison system. The one state prison in Milleredgeville held only 128 convicts total in 1852.

In 1862, for instance, only 28 inmates were sent to prison in the whole state during the year. But by 1870, after the 13th amendment to the u.s. constitution permanently legalizing convicted labor, the state's prison system was booming. There were 329 New Afrikans leased out to the Western & Atlantic Railroad for the back-breaking work of track grading. As well as 65 unlucky settler men there in separate gangs. While only 7 inmates were left behind inside the old prison. Matters only expanded from there.

The actual numbers re-enslaved were much higher, of course. Although social scientists mysteriously admit that there is no idea of how many New Afrikans were in post-Civil War "involuntary servitude" (what the patriarchal capitalist ruling class doesn't want us to know, their professors rarely investigate), there are concrete reasons for that. Tracing statistics already collected in lease contracts and other documents within the state government archives is one thing, but auctioning off criminalized New Afrikans was happening at county courthouses throughout the South. Not just for the big bosses, for plantations, mines, railroads, and timber extraction. Also as child labor for settler housewives, laborers for local small settler businesses, and bent over tending vegetable gardens and livestock at settler residences.

Conditions for convict laborers were terrible, of course, since they started off from the conditions that patriarchal capitalism had thought best for its en-slaved colony. Only in many cases worse, since purchasing chattel slavery's subjects under life sentence had always been expensive. While buying the lease of an arrested New Afrikan woman's labor for a fixed term of months or years was very cheap. So cheap that their survival was unimportant. Often, the settler employers permitted no distinction between male and female convicts. In 1883, the Texas State Convention of Negroes, "strongly condemned ... the practice of yoking or chaining male and female convicts together."

New Afrikan women might be yoked with a man, pulling farm machinery or a wagon in place of an ox or horse. Just as they might be chained together all day at labor, having to move with each other to the edge of the field to relieve themselves. And sometimes sleeping together in a group all crowded together in chains in a large cage or locked shed at night. The public controversies over the extreme conditions often obscured the issue of colonialism and human rights even more basic to their situation.

When i say that this state terrorism of the prison gulag and re-enslavement was necessary to put down the massive New Afrikan women's strike which had crippled the ex-Confederate economy, it wasn't just about dollars and cents. A war for the highest stakes was being fought out, in many forms, by everyone. Women and children, young and old, were in the war, too. **One thing that got revealed pretty quickly was that settler women and New Afrikan women were fighting it out between themselves on their social terrain, too.**

As long as we're on the subject of slavery, we should never ever forget that it will never actually end. Not so long as patriarchal capitalism still exists. The attraction of unwaged labor, of use-up-and-dispose people, to bosses is so great within the profit culture that slavery will keep occurring and reoccurring. Spontaneously generating from the matrix of capitalist relations itself. Why there's so many millions of slaves scattered throughout the world today. As there probably still will be a hundred years from now, too, if patriarchal capitalism is still alive.

Back in the 1970s, one summer i had my three young kids in tow and was impatiently waiting for the tomato picking harvest to begin for migrant workers, in Florida City. Eager to see if there was other work available that early in the season, i was driving around in my old four-wheel drive truck with the friend who was with me. Following a lead about a farm labor camp, we drove deeper and deeper on dirt roads twisting into the rough country. Finally, we came to a clearing with a large farm in sight and right at the edge, a labor camp with small cinder block houses like the size of a cell. We parked and waited to see what was what, because the place was a bit off. Usually, migrant camps are full of noise and people and kids running around. This place was, like, dead.

At last an old New Afrikan man came out and walked over to our truck. After the usual hellos and all, he leaned closer and said, plainly: *"You should leave before they find you. This is a bad place."* We asked what he meant, but that's all he would say. He repeated himself with emphasis, and got out of sight. So we just put the truck into gear and hauled ass. Not knowing what it was but taking advice seemed good.

Couple months later, i saw on the tv news that the government had raided that remote camp. Turns out for many years the large settler family who owned the big farm had been keeping workers more or less as slave labor, giving them booze but working them without wages and claiming they owed more and more for food and rent advances. They had been bused in by labor contractors. Then were really isolated and had trouble getting out. And never left with any pay. While the owner's sons walked around with guns on. Some of them had been there for years. Think that there's a lot more undiscovered slavery in the world than any of us ever want to see.

Of course, post-Civil War such re-slavery was carefully covered up and politely not acknowledged by Northern settler society.

Then, too, the captive labor by white men of Indian or indigenous peoples was still perfectly legal and common on the Western frontier. A white historian's account of why the "savage" Apache attacked u.s. settlers in the Southwest, calmly tells us:

> "More than anything else, it was probably the incessant kidnapping and enslavement of their women and children that gave Apaches their mad-dog enmity towards the whites … It was officially estimated that 2,000 Indian slaves were held by the white people of New Mexico and Arizona in 1866, after 20 years of American rule—unofficial estimates placed the figure several times higher … 'Get them back for us,' Apaches begged an Army officer in 1871, referring to 29 children just stolen by citizens of Arizona; 'our little boys will grow up slaves, and our little girls, as soon as they are large enough, will be diseased prostitutes, to get money for whoever owns them …' Prostitution of captured Apache girls, of which much mention is made in the 1860s and 1870s, seemed to trouble the Apaches exceedingly."

From what i've heard, Native or indigenous slavery finally ended inside the u.s. empire, though not completely until the 1960s. Until then, for example, the Aleut people on certain islands off Alaska were technically not slaves, but couldn't leave their islands without individual official u.s. permission. And there had to labor for the u.s. government as their sole employer, which sounds a lot like forced labor. They didn't have things like mail or drivers licenses or voting rights or local government or freedom of travel or … you get the picture. Is it slavery or is it Memorex?

And then we get to women as a gender-class, back then. The widest circle of all. How many of us, whether european settlers or whomever, were en-slaved? And not in some verbal turn of phrase, either. You notice how phrases like "domestic slavery" were crafted by patriarchy to actually mean the opposite, to be jokes that weren't funny, to be a bondage that was so uniquely trivialized that to men it was like having a more useful pet animal. Slavery as in forced to labor with our bodies whether in childbirth & raising children for the capitalist society, or in performing sex for the men who supervised us; or in domestic labor in the "home" that really was the factory for a new labor force as far as capitalism was concerned. In living memory that was life as it was known to many millions of women here. **And may be again, as it is for the majority of women in the world.**

That bloody u.s. Civil War between loyal and rebel settlers in the 19th century, was only one war of many within patriarchal capitalism. To play it again: What's true is that then as now there were wars related to more wars, seemingly without end; a mixed solar system of interrelated classes and clashing combatants. In which women of the varied nations and peoples and races were players, too.

Many settlers back then wondered what the rush to a bloody "civil war of brothers" was, anyway? Euro-settler capitalists from Ben Franklin and George Washington onward had been bitterly wrangling but compromising over Afrikan chattel slavery.

From long before the very incorporation of "America Inc." in 1776. This had been going on for over a hundred years, so why not compromise some more? Just kick the issue off again into the future as someone else's problem, many settlers from all classes wondered?

The reason is that the issue had run straight into a concentration of other wars, and had blown sky-high like a trainload of dynamite encountering a forest fire on one side and an artillery barrage on the other. Throughout the 1850s, the New Afrikan freedom struggle had been breaking through all restraints. What were once solitary escapes from this prison-plantation or that, had turned into larger and larger jailbreaks in the states near the Northern borders. More frequent, more dangerous. Often by groups armed and ready for a fight to the death. There was nothing "civil" about that war. There weren't any "brothers" at odds in those jailbreaks.

That is, the permanent state of war between u.s. patriarchal capitalism and its involuntary New Afrikan colony had reached a nodal point of change, dialectically. Moving abruptly into a new period. Southern prison-capitalists couldn't stand still anymore, tactically or strategically. They had to reassert military dominance in a stronger way over all the affected territory. For in that war, New Afrikan advances had run the Southern prison-capitalists clear out of any room for "compromise."

And in the larger strategic context, this issue still unresolved was interfering with the relentless westward expansion of amerikkka. The old Southwest of Texas, New Mexico, and California had been brought violently into the Union by the 1846–48 war to seize much of Mexico. Which itself caused considerable internal political unrest among settlers, particularly over the apparent strengthening of the Slave States' economy by the addition of slaver Texas into the u.s. empire.

But the future migration of a large enough mass of euro-settlers to hold down this region—the entire Northern 40%

of Mexico—was questionable; that is, if future Southern-style ranches, plantations, and businesses using New Afrikan captive labor monopolized the jobs and farming there. So the Civil War was always intertwined with other wars and larger arenas of conflict.

It wasn't just a competition about jobs or farmland. The expansion westward of the Slavery System endangered the whole u.s. empire, because there were two other factors involved. One thing obscured today is that most settlers in the North wanted and expected New Afrikans to die out completely, by any means necessary. In their view, it was the foolhardy and selfish prison-capitalists of the South who were artificially keeping four million extremely dangerous Afrikans alive right in the middle of what must become a "God-given" white men's paradise stretching from the Atlantic to the Pacific. In the settler men's debates about their constitution, when a Southern delegate said that their Afrikan prison-laborers were not people but merely property "like sheep," the sarcastic Benjamin Franklin from Philadelphia replied: "Sheep will never make rebellion."

"Stagecoach Mary" Fields, one of so many working-class New Afrikan women who charted their own path in the neo-colonial maelstorm. "Born a slave somewhere in Tennessee, Mary lived to become one of the freest souls ever to draw a breath, or a .38."

Even the leader of the "Silent Six," the ruling class men who were John Brown's hidden financial backers in his 1859 armed expedition to set the Slave South aflame, believed that "the Black man must die out" everywhere in amerikkka. Ending the economy of en-slaved racial labor was seen as a key toward this goal. During the middle of the Civil War, more than a few settler leaders were fixed on this. President Abraham Lincoln, for instance, wrote secretly to one of his generals:

> "I can hardly believe that the South and North can live in peace unless we get rid of the Negroes. Certainly they cannot, if we don't get rid of the Negroes whom we have armed and disciplined and who have fought with us, I believe, to the amount of 150,000 men. I believe it would be better to export them all ..."

In those euro-centric views, the expansion westward of the Slavery System was extremely dangerous to white society. In the first place, because it greatly expanded the already large number of New Afrikans inside the u.s. empire. And instead of being relatively isolated, as in the old South, westward expansion of the New Afrikan population brought them directly into contact with both Mexican and Native societies. All of whom were enemy peoples to the u.s. empire, no matter how many peace treaties Washington had drafted up and signed. Potentially bringing enemies together with enemies.

Remember that open wars and unsettled violent conflicts with hundreds of different Native nations and peoples were going on all over the outer boundaries of the u.s. empire's expansion. Ahead lay not only the famous Plains Indian War against the Comanche, Cheyenne, Lakota Sioux, and more, but also wars and continuing skirmishes and "policing" with the Apache, Bannock, Ute, and many others. While the Puget Sound War of 1855–56 had temporarily established euro-capitalist rule over the Puyallup, Klickitat, Nisqually, and other Native peoples in that area of the Northwest, in the Plains and Southwest nothing had been resolved yet. In fact, right

during the u.s. Civil War, in 1863–1865 the Union army together with settler armed gangs was fighting the Colorado
War against the Arapaho and Cheyenne. Fighting in the
Southwest with the Apache didn't officially end until 1886,
and small conflicts flared up until 1920. And the so-called
"Last Indian Uprising," a minor conflict with the Ute in Utah,
was in March 1923.

These were wars not merely of empire, but of truly different
cultures and social systems and environments. More than a
few, of cultures as incompatible to cash nexus agriculture and
industrial ku klux klanism as water is to iron. That's why Civil
War "hero" George Custer, after he accepted his Western army
commission leading the newly formed 7th Cavalry towards the
historic fame of Little Big Horn, had publicly promised to wipe
out what he insisted on calling the "red nyghers" of the Plains
Indians.

Ironically, Custer originally had been offered a first big
promotion to colonel by the u.s. war department, if he would
lead the 10th Cavalry Regiment of "colored troopers" against
the Plains Indian nations. Custer refused, insisting that the
"Buffalo soldiers" were naturally cowardly, and that he could
only conquer the Indians if given white men to command. We
could say that he made his own bed and then had to lie in it.

Not only were there indigenous cultures which didn't recognize property ownership in the capitalist sense, but societies
with different and much stronger women's cultures shaping
them. Different indigenous and settler sources dispute how
Custer finally got what was coming to him, but the Northern
Cheyenne have an oral history that has an edginess i like.
They say that day a well known woman warrior of their people
named Buffalo Calf Road Woman, was fighting at close quar-
ters against the 7th Cavalry at the Little Big Horn. The tribal
historians said that she was known for her martial skill, and
that it was her blow that knocked General Custer off his horse
and directly led to his death.

Women-led New Afrikan resistance produced a sudden realignment within the u.s. empire after 1865, of which the previously mentioned re-enslavement through imprisonment and convict leasing was just one cruel blow. **Now there were new ku klux klan thugs and new u.s. government agents working together side by side to force those women back into the unfree agricultural proletariat.**

Like a reflexive muscular backlash in the euro-settler culture. That new independence by freedwomen was answered with violence both spontaneous and strategic. Violence in homes, on the streets, on the job, by white women no less than white men, by criminal gangs as well as by government officials and courts. This euro-settler "leaderless conspiracy" had as its goal the mass terrorization and coercion of New Afrikan women, children, and men. To drive them as far back towards slavery as possible.

How could this be anything less than war? What the u.s. empire wanted to do to the New Afrikan Nation was far more than what they were willing to do to German Nazis. Much more than GIs are doing tonight in whatever country they are currently assaulting. By what measurement was that re-enslavement not war?

In a far too-common experience, when Lucretia Adams of Yorkville, S.C. was raped by a gang of eight white men, she was told: *"We heard you wouldn't work. We were sent for ... to come here and whip you, to make the damned niggers work."* Gang rape was often used then as now as an instrument of pro-u.s. government political terrorism. When Rhoda Ann Childs and her husband had finished the harvest of 1866 and asked for their pay, the white woman plantation owner refused. Instead of promised wages, she had a gang of nightriders kidnap and torture and rape Rhoda. "During the whipping one of the men had run his pistol into me, and said he had a mind to pull the trigger," she later told u.s. authorities.

Federal records from the u.s. Freedmen's Bureau contain countless complaints like these.

The u.s. government was and is the major author of the terrorism against New Afrikans. It has never been any "friend" to New Afrikan women. When somebody who is your enemy pretends to protect you, it's just another form of attack. Patriarchal capitalism never intended to let New Afrikan women escape being agricultural labor for them.

What New Afrikan women did back then was courageous beyond our experience today. It was strong and brilliant and a breakthrough. It threw the oppressor back for a beat, but it was not enough. Without a military strategy and an economic strategy, the attempt at separation broke down and could not develop.

A white deputy sherriff was trying to arrest Laura Nelson for stealing food; he was shot dead, allegedly by her son. Laura Nelson was raped before she and her son were lynched by a white mob on May 25, 1911, in Okemah, Oklahoma.

A Post-Civil War Conspiracy Theory

One of the biggest phony conspiracy theories in u.s. history came out of this situation. It is the white liberal story that Black Reconstruction's downfall was due to a supposed conspiracy by white racists to terrorize their way back into power across the South. Aided, they say with crocodile tears, by the hesitation of the "good people" of the North who still compromised on New Afrikan human rights. Outgunned and outnumbered by the new klan and the ex-Confederate tide, according to this phony conspiracy theory, New Afrikans in state after state had no choice but to surrender before the overpowering racist conspiracy. Blah, blah, blah. Haven't you heard something along these lines? Even in college "Black studies" classes and from dissenters? All a patchwork fabric of half-truths and things torn out of context, of course. Not true at all, not by half. That's why they've pasted this mess into their euro-capitalist his-story books to forcefeed into children's minds.

Within such a conspiracy theory is planted a poisonous seed. It murmurs subliminally over and over that New Afrikan people are just vics, not able enough to hold their own against other races. Or too weak mentally to keep from getting beaten up by white settlers again and again. Patriarchal capitalist civilization plants these disabling ideas as part of mental colonization, as chains of falsehood for the mind.

It doesn't take long to run down the facts. Let's start with the outnumbered part. **New Afrikans actually weren't outnumbered by the ex-Confederates.** There was the famous plantation "Black Belt," the wide zone of contiguous counties with over fifty percent New Afrikan population that stretched from Louisiana across the South to the Atlantic. Moreover, the White South was devastated and in ruins after the Civil War. Once the most powerful region of the u.s. empire, the South had lost one out of every four white men of military age. Forty percent of their livestock were gone, along with half of their farm machinery and thousands of miles of railroad track. Farms, houses, mills, warehouses, and businesses stood in ruins or just abandoned all over the South. Their position was so weakened that many defeated ex-Confederate men gave up & emigrated westward to the Indian frontier. To become real white men over people of color again. So the ex-Confederates themselves were on the ropes.

In many cases it was the planter capitalists who were the ones terrorized, as was only to be expected. Even when New Afrikans were still en-slaved, white Southerners despite all their arrogant talk, lived in fear of what they might do. One Georgia woman said that their slaves were "a threatening source of constant insecurity, and every Southern *woman* to whom I have spoken on the subject, has admitted to me that they live in terror of their slaves." (Her emphasis). A Louisiana plantation owner recalled periods "when there was not a single planter who had a calm night's rest; they then never lay down to sleep without a brace of pistols at their side."

During the Civil War, at first the Confederates insisted on holding captured soldiers of the Black Regiments for later return to their original plantation owners. But very soon they realized that the new flood of New Afrikan troops meant sure defeat for them. The Confederate army out of its fear and desperation, turned to terrorism. All captured New Afrikan soldiers were to be treated as rebellious slaves and slaughtered, to try and break the morale of the new regiments. At the infamous battle of Poison Spring, on April 18, 1864, some 600 captured men of the 1st Kansas Colored Infantry were shot and beaten to death. A few days before that, Confederate General Nathan Bedford Forrest's cavalry had captured the Union's Fort Pillow in Tennessee, killing over a hundred surrendering New Afrikan soldiers. There the Confederates also buried wounded New Afrikan soldiers alive, and slaughtered all accompanying Black civilians including women and children. That was an act of deliberate terrorism, ordered by Confederate commanders.

That was also a serious mistake by the "ole Dixie" army. Because the Black Regiments then swore to take no more Confederate prisoners until their people, soldier & civilian alike, were equally respected. This is seldom reported, naturally. On April 30, 1864, for example, men of the brother 2nd Kansas Colored Infantry cut off and overran a Confederate artillery position, killing every Confederate including the wounded and surrendered. Then they went looking for more surrendered Confederates after a nearby battle. One of the Confederate physicians there complained later: *"Many of our wounded had been mutilated in many ways. Some with ears cut off, throats cut … One officer wrote on a piece of paper that his lower jaw and tongue were shot off after the battle was over."* Yes, the trash-talking white Southerners started living in fear of the Black Regiments, and for good reason.

For instance, at the later battle for Mobile, Alabama, in April 1865, a New Afrikan infantry division stormed the Confederate lines and broke through, crying *"Remember Fort Pillow!"* The terrorized Confederates broke and ran for their lives, in most cases unsuccessfully. Many tried to swim away and were drowned or shot down. Others ran in panic towards white Union units, begging to be taken as captives. A settler Union officer wrote his family: *"The niggers did not take a prisoner, they killed all they took to a man."* So the euro-capitalist propaganda picture of New Afrikans back then cowered into inaction because of their fear of bullying white men, is just racist crap.

Nor were New Afrikans unarmed or even outgunned at first. New Afrikan women and men were already fighting for what they knew was theirs. On the Sea Islands off the Carolina coast, plantation after plantation abandoned by fleeing Confederates early on in the Civil War had been seized. 40,000 New Afrikans divided up the land amongst them. Armed people's patrols guarded the seashore there, waiting to repel the planters that they knew would be trying to sneak back into their Big Houses. When the planters returned to the Islands after the Civil War, they were met by groups of New Afrikans who "coolly told returning planters to go—and pulled out weapons to emphasize their orders." This was happening throughout the South. Near Hampton, Virginia, some 5,000 New Afrikans had divided up plantations between them, and their leaders carried "revolvers, cutlasses, carbines, and shotguns" to hold onto liberated lands. In all these cases, the armed New Afrikans were overcome in the end not by any Southerners, but by the white Union Army.

Who had the armed ascendancy right after the Civil War depended on the specific location; it varied widely. Where the euro-settlers had a population and organizational advantage, as was true even in many areas in Mississippi and Louisiana, the white paramilitary gangs ruled outright. But in many other areas New Afrikans greatly outnumbered the depleted settlers, and there the story was different. Though seldom told, as it might give the oppressed dangerous ideas.

For example, in the profitable but harsh rice plantation areas right outside Savannah, Georgia, by the 1868 elections the local euro-capitalists had retaken the government through crude fraud and violence. Winked at by the Federal government. Yet, the roads leading from the city into the rice marshes were still patrolled regularly by several New Afrikan volunteer armed militias, the Union League of ex-soldiers and the Home Guards. The Federal Freedman's Bureau representatives had forced the Black workers to accept labor contracts giving them only one-third of the proceeds from the rice crop at year's end. Angry, the workers refused to abide by the contracts, and swore to have the land or their just share of the crop, if they had to "fight knee-deep in blood."

In a series of night raids in late December, armed New Afrikans overcame white watchmen and supervisors on plantations, and transported some six thousand bushels of rice out of the planters' warehouses. Loaded onto boats, the sacks of rice were moved to hiding places on the river. On

December 23, 1868, Sheriff James Dooner with two deputies and a complaining planter, J. Middleton, arrived in the area with warrants for the arrest of seventeen New Afrikans. The main militant New Afrikan leader in Savannah, Solomon Farley, was one of those to be arrested.*

Arresting Farley without resistance, the party headed for the train station to return to Savannah. However, waiting for them at the station was an angry demonstration of several hundred New Afrikans, many armed with guns and axes and clubs. The large number of New Afrikan women were what frightened the Sheriff the most: *"... all jabbering together like a pack of magpies. They were striking the ground with sticks, flourishing them in the air, and other things of that kind."* And when he tried to talk to them, they refused to listen. Saying, *"We don't care for the sheriff, neither for the state of Georgia, the Governor, nor for the President of the United States. We have our own laws here."*

Finally, the Sheriff's small party decided it was safer to surrender to the men of the Home Guards, commanded by Captain Green, which took their guns, warrants, and money, and directed them to return to Savannah on foot. The next day, the shaken Sheriff Dooner, reinforced with twenty settler men with rifles, returned on a railroad train. After much gunfire on the settlers' part, they quickly retreated back to the city saying that the Black insurgents had them too greatly outnumbered. At night the New Afrikan militias continued taking over the district, emptying barns and burning down planters' houses. The revolt was finally ended when the New Afrikan militias agreed to surrender. However, only to Federal officials, not state or local forces. In early January 1869, two companies of u.s. army infantry took control of this rice district, arresting by agreement 68 New Afrikans for a major political trial in Savannah.

---

* Farley was elected to political offices that the white government would refuse to let him occupy, and later in exile became the first New Afrikan lawyer in Brooklyn, N.Y.

The trials of the armed insurgents, which promised so much drama, fizzled since all sides decided to call it a draw. The raided planters ended up testifying, in effect, for the defense, downplaying the conflict. They wanted to reach some accommodation with the New Afrikan laborers, upon whom their business depended. The result was not even, of course. The euro-settler businessmen retained control of Savannah and the region. The planters held onto their estates. The New Afrikan workers kept their vows and largely refused to labor in the rice fields, except on a part-time or casual basis. Most especially the New Afrikan women. Buying or renting small bits of former plantation land, they survived by vegetable gardening, fishing, selling handicrafts, and casual labor.

Despite desperate attempts at using Irish or South American or even Chinese imported laborers, the planters were largely forced out of rice farming. Once so profitable, Georgia's rice plantations saw their share of total u.s. rice production fall from roughly 25% to less than 5% by the end of the 1800s. They were replaced themselves, in effect, by the plantation owners of Louisiana. The imprint of the proletarian rebellion was long-lasting. New Afrikan workers, unable to take the land and the agricultural industry that was theirs, forced the business collapse of their capitalist foes.

Cockspur Island, Georgia, 1863

The Union Army's Black Regiments, as occupiers in the first months after the Civil War, spontaneously became just as radical in deeds as the later 1960s Black Panthers. In county after county, emptying out the plantation's Big House in a party atmosphere. Dividing the food and clothing and furniture up, in a "festival of the oppressed." Sometimes driving off the local white police, freeing prisoners from jails. Backing up New Afrikans who went on strike for higher wages or who had seized property that their unwaged labor had built. Even patrolling town streets with rifles in hand to keep the infiltrating white power down. Far from being outgunned or passive, men of the Black Regiments had a good idea of what it would take to stay free and were doing it. Until the u.s. government became alarmed.

On the advice of Gen. U.S. Grant, commanding the Union army, the Whitest House ordered the Black regiments all disbanded. Confederate soldiers were allowed to disperse and go home keeping their weapons and ammunition. While the Black regiments usually had their rifles taken from them before the men were discharged. Not a small difference to poor people.

The u.s. media always blurs the difference between two very different groups of 19th century New Afrikan soldiers in Union blue. The Black Regiments of the war to end the Slavery System were one thing, but the later "Buffalo Soldiers" were something completely different. The Black Regiments were completely disbanded relatively soon after the Civil War ended. Too dangerous to let stay around locked and loaded.

Later, needing mercenaries to protect the wagon trains of racist euro-settlers invading Native lands, in 1866 the u.s. Congress authorized the recruiting of new Black units who would be confined to the Western frontier. Just for that colonizing purpose. The new 9th and 10th Cavalry Regiments were formed out of Ft. Leavenworth, Kansas, with two supporting regiments of Black infantry being formed at other bases. Recruiting for the Indian wars in the West was a hard sell, and was personally done by the regiments' few officers traveling to cities like St. Louis and Philadelphia.

Most of the "Buffalo soldiers" were young unemployed workers, who were cheap and disposable. Willing to commit crimes of empire in return for proving their manhood, as well as having a gun to carry and "three squares and a cot." Theirs were the mercenary units that carried the brunt of the fighting for years to conquer Indian societies in the West. Because their units were on permanent duty in the West year after year, while the euro-settler army units all got rotated back East after only a year or two, the "Buffalo soldiers" became the most experienced combat veterans in the whole u.s. military. But using their abilities only against other oppressed people of color. That's why the capitalist cultural machinery to this day always wants to mislead us into confusing the two.

When the white nightriders did appear in the South, they were in many cases easily driven off at first by local New Afrikan militia companies, where they had survived. Such as the famous one briefly led by Captain Charles Caldwell in Mississippi before his assassination. Far from their fearsome reputation later on, the klan, white caps, white legion, and other ex-Confederate paramilitaries made a record of cowardice and military incompetence whenever they faced any organized opposition. Just as Robert E. Lee's Confederate troops in gray uniforms had earlier established new records in fleeing and deserting. New Afrikan militias and self-defense associations had an almost universal record of victory after victory against the white gangs. But these militias were restrained or disbanded by white state governments, while regular u.s. army detachments in blue would appear to repress New Afrikan strikes and land takeovers.

Nor was there any white racist conspiracy. "Because conspiracy means secret plans, secret organization, secret activities," while nothing was really secret there. In those rural communities and towns, you don't think that everyone didn't know what was going on, and by who? Or even in the cities? The klan and the later lynch mobs were formed under the leadership of "the best men" in town after town. Planters, bankers, politicians, and big businessmen, these were the leaders coordinating the insurgency.

The klan itself quickly grew, helped by the publicity of using the name of the famed Confederate general Nathan Bedford Forrest as their first publicly elected Grand Wizard. Who claimed to the white public that the klan had organized 500,000 members throughout the South, and that he personally could call out 5,000 armed klansmen to his side on short notice. Hardly out of plain sight. Leadership councils and tactical operations were held in secret, of course, just as in any capitalist enterprise. And public deniability was maintained both to spin the terminally gullible, and as a legal protection for individual terrorist leaders and members. But everyone knew what was happening who wanted to know.

Ex-Confederates James George and L. Lamar led the infamous "Mississippi Plan," which mapped out the systematic killing of all Black activists throughout the state. Then the hijacking of elections and state government. Their big reputations as state leaders of the violent ex-Confederate insurgency led the local power structure and the white voters to reward both of them with becoming u.s. Senators.

In the last bloody stages of the ex-Confederate takeover, Ida B. Wells was to publicly scorn the idea of "trusting in the law" to imprison white assassins and lynch mob leaders in Memphis, Tennessee. Since, as she said, the criminal court judge who would try them, the newspaper publisher who would expose them, and the police chief who would repress them were all well known to be among the terrorist leaders themselves. There were no secret conspiracies in real life there. Just like right now.

Here we see conspiracy theories at their most negative. To cover for & excuse away the major role played by the

**new capitalist neo-colonial African-American "mislead-
ership" class.** Just like in our time, as so many have com-
mented. The fantasy about unstoppable klan conspiracies was
spread to cover for something else: the u.s. ruling class ma-
nipulation of the newly promoted Negro patriarchs to disable
New Afrikan communities from within. So that they could be
re-enslaved in one-sided warfare. Even by shoot-in-the-back
types as cowardly as the ex-Confederates.

For the first time, the patronage of the u.s. government and
the ruling euro-settler political party were used to create an actual neo-colonial middle-class. Which became the core of the
"Black bourgeoisie." Robert Smalls is a good example. He had
been a Civil War hero and became the first African-American
u.s. congressman from South Carolina. In 1876, plantation
workers in his state rebelled, taking over rural areas in a general strike and then defeating the local white police in battles.
Congressman Smalls personally accompanied the settler state
militia in to disarm the militants. He then led the New Afrikan
community back into voluntarily restoring white power over
themselves. This is a neo-colonial job description that has per-
sisted to this very day.

Dr. Martin Delany was a pioneering nationalist who published a national anti-slavery newspaper with escapee Frederick
Douglass, the famous Abolitionist leader. Delany had been appointed as the first New Afrikan major of infantry in the u.s.
army. He had even won president Lincoln's personal approval
to try and form an irregular "Black Legion" for the Union in
the Civil War. Again, his impressive talents were put to use after the War in governing his people for the Freedmen's Bureau.

But in December 1865, Major Delany was recalled to active
service by the Union Army *"for important special duty."*
Commanding a unit of u.s. troops, Delany toured the Sea
Island plantations to report on widespread rumors of an uprising planned for the xmas holidays. His armed cavalry were a
show of force to back up speeches convincing the people to

disarm and give up any goals of holding onto farmlands. His people, Major Delany spelled out in his community talks, must go back to being hard workers for the euro-settler business and plantation owners. This newly invented type of African-American neo-colonial leadership was happening throughout the South.

Frederick Douglass was the most widely respected New Afrikan leader back then, the equivalent of the Rev. Martin Luther King, Jr. in the 1960s. Unlike Dr. King, Douglass was rewarded with government positions, including even as a diplomat. Once a carpenter bound day and night in chattel slavery, Douglass escaped and rose to the position of u.s. consul in Haiti. A storybook rise beyond even Barack Obama's.

Angela Davis has written an entire essay just on Douglass and his class dilemma over convict labor, connecting the dots between their cooptation and the puzzling lack of effective Black opposition to convict labor. In *From the Prison of Slavery to the Slavery of Prison: Frederick Douglass and the Convict Lease System*, she notes that Douglass said that he hadn't really known about the convict labor injustice at first. By which he meant for almost twenty years. It wasn't until 1881 that he

Martin Delany

Frederick Douglass

first began to publicly voice any criticism at all over the re-enslavement going on.

The dirty deal of the corrupt Hayes-Tilden Compromise had been reached in 1877, between Northern and Southern capitalists, giving complete criminal control of the ex-Confederacy back to the white gangs and planter politicians. Douglass was completely neutralized in the crisis. As Angela Davis points out, *"In fact, just as President Rutherford B. Hayes decided to withdraw federal troops from the South, he also decided to appoint Frederick Douglass as U.S. Marshall of the District of Columbia."*

Not too coincidentally, Frederick Douglass put his great reputation *against* any grassroots movement for independence or even self-defense. He refused to organize against the wave of lynchings in the bold way that he had against Slavery earlier. Douglass said that he believed the story that the new phenomena of lynchings truly were the fault of lower class New Afrikan men. Who he believed had lusted to sexually attack white women.

While leading men of that period's "black bourgeoisie" were heavily criticized in retrospect for betrayal by 1960s revolutionaries, it would also be accurate to say that they had been coopted. Playing neo-colonial roles that had never been tried before. Because they were imprisoned within the interests and vision of their class. You can go against your family and you can go against your neighbors, but to go against your class is really hard.

Capitalist class agenda and class loyalty entered the arena then *inside* the New Afrikan Nation for the first time, decisively. **The newly minted African-American "misleadership" class after the Civil War did have a strategy.** Of proving the loyalty of people of color to the u.s. ruling class, and using that to lobby for the federal government to someday equalize themselves as an exceptional class. That is, they had a military strategy that was dependent on *someone else's* army, the u.s. army.

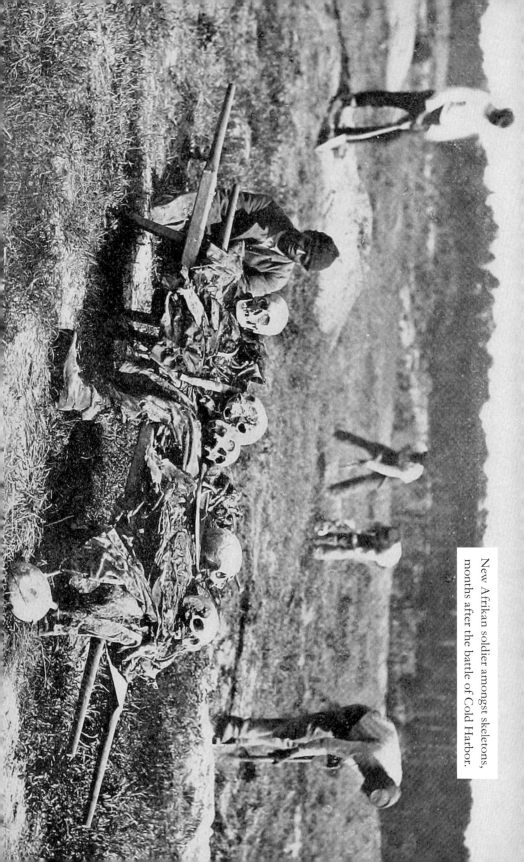

New Afrikan soldier amongst skeletons, months after the battle of Cold Harbor.

Scene in the New Afrikan quarter, Savannah, Ga., 1886.

Black Patriarchy vs. New Afrikan Communalism

This was a new male class whose privileged existence was only made possible by being part of the already congealed patriarchal capitalist civilization. Which they inescapably had to defend in order to join. They carried out this agenda of their own class in its faithful-lieutenant role with the higher u.s. ruling class, which had, after all, made their own existence possible. That it had devastating effects on their own people no doubt troubled them, and had to be rationalized away in their minds. Like the evils of drug trafficking are shrugged off by the lumpen gang leaders today.

The creation of African-American patriarchy was a conscious strategy of the euro-settler government. Specifically, to further control women in a personal way where they lived. New Afrikan society, just as the indigenous societies, was quite distinct from european models this way. Ironically, the planter and his wife and children in the "Big House" were completely unequal and culturally backward in every way, while among the New Afrikan women and men in the prison shacks women were more than equal. At a time when euro-settler women had no right to divorce, New Afrikan women could divorce their voluntary partners simply. Since women were more likely than men to have escaped being "sold away," they were more likely than men to be the sages who led a captive community. Although both genders fulfilled those roles.

All the forces of capitalist culture, the u.s. government no less than the banks and the klan, acted back then to push New Afrikan women down under New Afrikan men. For the specific purpose of stifling their rebelliousness and stopping their withholding of plantation labor. It became an official goal of the Freedmen's Bureau, the new federal agency responsible for regulating ex-captives, to make a Black patriarchy for the first time in the u.s. New Afrikan women's hold on farmland was often denied or reduced because of their gender-class. New Afrikan women's wages were officially set by the u.s. government at less than men's. Just like among euro-settlers. Discrimination in hiring and firing against New Afrikan single mothers with children was legalized; there were tragic cases of infanticide after desperate women had been threatened by bosses that if they had another child to feed they would be fired.

For the first time New Afrikan men were designated as the dominant "head of family" in all official dealings. Their new adoption of the amerikkkan nuclear family was specifically as appointed labor overseers of rebellious women. "For example, the Cuthbert, Georgia, U.S. Freedmen's Bureau official made one man promise *'to work faithfully and keep his wife in subjection'* after the woman refused to work and 'Damned the Bureau' ...'" Federal agent DeForest in South Carolina instructed men: *"They must make their wives and daughters work."*

Patriarchal capitalism gave recognition to men as the only negotiators for their people. Whether it was the political party or the plantation owner, the police or the bank. This instantly put more weight on the male side of New Afrikan society. There was an obvious dual consciousness, of tactically going along with the new rules or of buying into the ego-filling role of "master of the house." A settler woman who taught New Afrikan children in South Carolina wrote privately that the new African-American male leadership was urging all the men *"to get the woman into their proper place—never tell them anything of their concerns, etc., and the notion of being bigger than women generally is now inflating the conceit of the males to an amazing degree."* It is interesting that as a sideline, the new ku klux klan started making late night visits to New Afrikan homes to order that women and men who were living together must enter into xtian marriage. The patriarchal family was a link in the chain to the klan, too.

This ran all over the communal non-authoritarian culture that New Afrikan women, children, and men had nurtured underground. A culture in which helping each other survive and sharing were constants. A culture in which women & men both gave leadership and tried to be self-reliant.

A small but enduring symbol of that women's communal self-reliance was the Combahee River women's community. Several hundred women from the Combahee River area of South Carolina took over plantation land during the Civil War, and started their own women's agricultural colony. The "Combees," as they were known, grew cotton and potatoes, gathered groundnuts, raised children together, and sustained themselves in the middle of the War. They also produced winter socks and scarves and other gear for the soldiers in the 2nd South Carolina Colored Volunteers.

This communal culture of the oppressed was definitely a form of political struggle. Union officials saw this women's communalism of those who had nothing as a threat to the hegemony of capitalist values, with its self-centered individualism. Freedmen Bureau agent DeForest was only typical in instructing New Afrikans to think first of getting ahead for themselves, not of helping others: *"He pointed to the case of Aunt Judy, a black laundress who barely eked out a living for herself and her small children. Yet she had 'benevolently taken in, and was nursing, a sick woman of her own race ... The thoughtless charity of this penniless Negress in receiving another povery-stricken creature under her roof was characteristic of the Freedmen.'"* The euro-settler agents trying to supervise New Afrikan society thought that this was a negative, not a positive.

New Afrikan women were targeted for attack because their traditional communal culture with gender equality and many woman-centered families was a dangerous breakout. And had to be attacked, to at least contain it, before the model of this anti-patriarchal, anti-capitalist example spread.

Because it has always been suppressed in patriarchal capitalist culture, New Afrikan women's communality has always had a fugitive existence. As is true for women everywhere still.

152

But it never goes away. So deeply was this woman-centered survival culture rooted in New Afrikan life that despite an entire encrustation of white and Black male supremacy on top of it, it has survived from one generation to the next (and still survives today) in the daily lives of millions of women and children.

For instance, to take a detour and jump forward to a different time for a beat, just to mention one spectacular example of this. During the great difficulties of the 1930s Depression, New Afrikan women's communalism came to the surface in many different forms. Often clothed in religion. The Peace Mission church of Father Divine was exceptional in that it didn't hide this woman-centered communality as usually happened, but openly built on it. Attracting strategically more support for just this reason.

Father Divine's church claimed millions of followers in the 1930s, but it was believed that its actual membership was roughly 30,000–50,000 then. It was famous for two things. First, there were Father Divine's eccentric mix of doctrines: that he personally was god; that race and gender were only surface illusions of people who were all equal and the same. And secondly, but most importantly, that the culture could be taken apart and put back together very differently into celibate communes to reflect this. The 1960s counter-culture had nothing on Father Divine. Instead of stripped down soup kitchens like today's charities, the working-class New Afrikan women who were the main activists in that church organized huge fifty-course banquets in a Harlem hall, lavishly decorated and open to all.

Unemployed Harlemites were fed by the women organizers of the Peace Mission, which created millions of dollars in new cooperative businesses to meet basic needs during those very worst times. They would hold gigantic mass banquets, open to all in the Harlem main base of the church. Where the eager donations of those who had a few greenbacks paid for those who had no money and were fed for very little or sometimes for free. In Louise Meriwether's semi-autobiographical novel of girlhood in the difficult poverty of 1930s Harlem, *Daddy Was a Numbers Runner*, 12-year-old Francie wants a "good" week, when she'll have a quarter for herself. That means she can dine at the Peace Mission and fill herself with such wonderful food.

One religion student ate there regularly in 1945, long after the peak of this movement's strength, and still was amazed at what was put before him (we quote his record of the banquets in full, just to preserve the impact of this surprising operation):

"Eleven different cooked vegetables passed in quick succession: steamed rice, green beans, boiled cabbage, sweet corn, succotash, stewed tomatoes, lima beans, greens, and carrots. I, not knowing what to expect, had begun by taking a little bit of everything but soon saw that this was not wise and became more selective. Then came platters of meat. It will be recalled that this experience was still in wartime and rationing had not yet been lifted. First came three or four cold cuts, including baked ham. Then appeared the hot, fresh cooked meats: roast beef, beef curry, meat loaf, fried chicken, roast duck, roast turkey, beef steak, each heaped high on the platters which were passed around the festive board. Then came the salads: fruit salad containing Persian melon, cantaloupe, alligator pears, and lettuce, and sliced tomato salad. Next came bread: hot corn bread, hot rolls, white bread, brown bread, rye bread, raisin bread, and for good measure, crackers, accompanied by a good serving of butter ... Dessert consisted of two kinds of cake, one of them with fruit and whipped cream. On another like occasion, great heaping bowls of ice cream of two or three different flavors were circulated around the table. Along with all this were sweet pickles, mixed pickles, ripe olives, green olives, and all the condiments that would ordinar-

154

ily be served on such an occasion. The average number of different dishes served at these banquets is around fifty-five."

It's an interesting contrast: those long ago communal feasts that New Afrikan women organized with and for the poor and hungry in Harlem during the 1930–40s; compared to the meals indifferently served or mostly not provided at all by the high-tech u.s. "Superpower" to captive New Orleans disaster refugees in the Superdome in 2005. Father Divine was the spiritual and political head, but in the New Afrikan tradition the organization was run and organized by women. The New Afrikan women organizers of the 1930s Peace Mission did much more than feed the hungry.

New Afrikan women there led anti-racist activity, anti-death penalty education, anti-fascist demonstrations, fighting for the right to vote, and other political causes. Racially mixed groups of Peace Mission women would demand service at segregated restaurants and other businesses. Some 80% of the members were women, mostly New Afrikan and working-class. Many of the most politically experienced of these women were veterans of Marcus Garvey's Pan-Afrikan mass nationalist movement in the 1920s. Father Divine may have been eccentric or enlightened, but what he figured out was that he could skim what he wanted from the river, so long as he remembered to step back and simply encourage New Afrikan working-class women to lead in creating things that had never existed before.

The Peace Mission's popularity among political New Afrikan women was a real eye-opener because Father Divine wasn't into rubber biscuits when it came to race and gender. Instead of little nuclear families, the thousands of New Afrikan women in the Peace Mission lived in supposedly celibate, racially-integrated "Heavens" with other women. These women-only households were also cooperative economic enterprises. And everyone in the Mission took new names, as is common in the

New Afrikan cultural tradition for major turning points, just like in the 1960s. Those whose names were stolen from them in history can turn a weakness into a strength. While some Peace Mission women gave themselves names like Joyful Rose, others took up men's names like Joshua Love.

Living in women's communes, without private property, men or individual childraising, was considered a scandal in the 1930s and 1940s u.s.a. On a practical level it temporarily created a suddenly enlarged space in those women's lives for new works of all kinds. When Father Divine suggested in 1935 that New Afrikan women could attend night classes at public schools to become literate, and thus able to register as voters, New Afrikan women suddenly became 20% of the night school students in New York City. Before then, no woman had attended night classes at Harlem's Public School 89 in ten years. The mass push towards education by New Afrikan women has broken out at more than one point in their her-story. It is going on right now, in what is obviously more than simply personal advancement but a wave of "advancing the Race."

Not only did those New Afrikan women in the 1930s and early 1940s cooperatively run bakeries and clothing stores and other retail businesses, but they started "the Promised Land." Which were almost seven hundred small household farms scattered around New York state. While the spectacle of hundreds of new women-only cooperative farms met with scorn and predictions of sure failure from the press, they did quite well by themselves. What the capitalist media had not understood was that working-class New Afrikan women born in the South usually had considerable experience with rural life and basic farming. This alternative culture church ran into considerable harassment from the government. And in any case did not survive the political stresses of World War II and the growing rightward conservatism of its charismatic male founder.

The communal politics in New Afrikan women's culture didn't die there either, of course. It only went underground again to re-emerge in other forms. The point is that women of the New Afrikan Nation were finding their own communal grassroots solutions in so many creative ways. Fighting by taking care of themselves has a rich her-story.

It is this clash in the daily lives of millions between patriarchy and communalism which still goes on.

Not that there wasn't widespread grassroots resistance of all kinds by both women and men during the fall of Black Reconstruction, even while disorganized and misled. The Band family were marked as targets because they were militant community leaders. A herstory says: "The klan came to his house, took his wife, hung her to a tree, hacked her to death with knives." Having escaped their raid, George Band ambushed the klan, killing fourteen of them with his Winchester rifle before fleeing into exile. Never caught. Or the Miller family from Kentucky, where Richard Miller's mother was simply abducted by an ex-Confederate after the War. Even though Slavery was supposed to be illegal, her settler kidnapper just took her to rural Texas and re-enslaved her. Finally, after years of searching, Richard Miller received a letter that his mother had managed to mail out. Going to Texas, he hunted down her abductor and killed him, and freed his mother. There were more than a few personal stories like that.

The her-storian Paula Giddings tells us: "... the economic struggle was a violent one, and now Black women would not only have to work as they had during slavery, but would again have to take up arms in defense of the race. Thus when whites threatened to regain power at the end of Reconstruction in Charleston, South Carolina, an eyewitness reported seeing Black women 'carrying axes or hatchets in their hands hanging down at their sides, their aprons or dresses half-concealing their weapons.' In rallying freedmen and women to defend their rights, a Black clergyman of the time could confidently boast of '80,000 black men in the State who can use Winchesters and 200,000 black women who can light a torch and carry a knife.'"

If there really were more New Afrikan women than men who were ready to go to war again right then & there, wouldn't have it made more sense to give *them* the Winchester rifles and let the men use the knives? This unthinking sexist outlook of making self-defense & war "men's business" was, practically speaking, as good as conceding defeat. And war is nothing if it not practical.

The old market at Lynchburg, VA

The Pedestal & the Gutter Can Both be the Same Address

The state terrorism of mass incarceration and "involuntary servitude" was not only about immediate capitalist greed. Actually-existing capitalism needed to reinforce its ku klux klan, to drive down and recapture New Afrikan women. Who were resisting and angling their way almost out of capitalism.

Want to double down, and underline what i said earlier: A war for the highest stakes was being fought out, in many forms, by everyone. Women and children, young and old, were in the war, too. One thing that got revealed pretty quickly was that settler women and New Afrikan women were fighting it out between themselves, too, on their terrain.

New Afrikan women stubbornly fought re-enslavement every step of the way into the early years of the 20th century. As the new "Jim Crow" laws mandated public segregation, New Afrikan women in twenty-five Southern cities organized boycotts to maintain their equal access to railroad travel. The leaders of euro-settler society had to issue public calls for even *more* violence by white men against New Afrikan women. They thought it especially dangerous that groups of New Afrikan women-children back then were refusing to do the "deference ritual" acknowledging white women as their superiors. Under segregation, white people demanded public rituals where Black people were supposed to always step aside when white people were using the sidewalk. Ducking or bowing the head with eyes averted to signal their servitude.

So it wasn't true that women and girl-children weren't embroiled in the thick of the fighting. They were, down and dirty. On *both* sides. When two nations are at war, oppressor versus oppressed, there really are no sidelines. That's just an oppressor illusion. It gets easier to see when we go beneath the "political" events and catch up with the issues of women's daily lives.

On 18 February, 1886, a bright and ambitious twenty-four-year-old schoolteacher in Memphis, Tennessee, wrote the details down in her diary about a recent court case: "for fear I will not remember it when I write my 'novel'." The settler judge had been severe. The defendant was a young "colored girl" convicted of assault. Her crime was that when on a daily walk on a "wooded path up the country," she had refused to give way in a "deference ritual" and let a white girl she regularly met coming the other way, have the whole path. The "colored girl" had insisted on her "half of the walk," even after the settler girl brought her brother one day who "abused" her. The next day the "colored girl" was ready and got "the best of a fight" with the settler girl. For winning fair and square, she was arrested like so many others and brought to trial. The schoolteacher wrote angrily in her diary that the judge "carried to the utmost of his power by giving her 11 mos. 29 days and ½ in the workhouse!"

The Memphis schoolteacher was Ida B. Wells, who would never find the spare time to write that novel. We know her anyway. And not because she was the first New Afrikan woman to make her living completely as a writer and publisher. Although she was that. But primarily because she became world famous. For almost single-handedly starting the movement against lynching in the South. Taking it first nationally and then internationally. She began what we now know as the modern civil rights movement in the u.s. empire. Ida B. Wells risked herself many times, and publicly carried the pistol that she said all Black women and men should have. Swearing to take some settler men with her, if and when she was finally lynched herself. Incredible but true, she was the foremother of the Rev. Martin Luther King, Jr., and in an essential way, Malcolm X, too.

Ida B. Wells didn't just sympathize with that New Afrikan girl who had been sentenced to a year at "involuntary servitude" for refusing to knuckle under to a white girl. She had been so caught by that story because she might well have been

that girl-child herself, when even younger. Fresh out of chattel slavery. As a very young girl right after the overthrow of the Confederacy, Ida B. Wells had gone to the new freedmen's school in her hometown of Holly Springs, Mississippi. The school and the young New Afrikan students had to fight for everything, including their right to walk on the town's sidewalks. Against the gangs of settler girls who were determined to physically shove them aside, to force them into obeying the "deference ritual" as supposed inferiors.

The diary of a local white woman records this clash in their daily lives with the New Afrikan schoolgirls: "... they marched all around town with the Yankee flag, and a standard-bearing inscription—The First Colored School in Holly Springs—Most of the girls went to see them, but I would not look at the things for anything." After school, when there would be right of way skirmishes with the settler girls and women, their teacher, who was a fierce Anti-Slavery advocate and the wife of a former Union officer, would join them. A local white herstorian said

that this white teacher "would place herself in the center of her black column of girls who would lock arms so as to form a solid wall across the sidewalk." Settlers would have to themselves give way and step aside or have to fight the whole "black column." They were not used to having the shoe put on the other foot.

We forget sometimes that the nature of euro-settler societies is that "every white man is a police, too." The *Chattanooga Times* newspaper in Tennessee, for example, urged its male readers to target such New Afrikan girl-children for immediate personal violence. Supposedly, in order to "defend" white women:

> *"Negro girls are apt to be extremely insolent, not only to whites of their own age but to ladies. In the matter of collisions between school-boys, that may best be left to the police. The negro girls who push white women and girls off the walks can be cured of that practice by the use of a horsewhip; and we advise white fathers and husbands to use the whip. It's a great corrective."*

This was the meaning of white women infamously being "put on a pedestal" by patriarchal capitalism. Not out of respect, as those slimy loser male cultures always half-pretend. From the Confederate prison-labor capitalists to today's Islamic Republic. But as propaganda to agitate for more hate crimes.

Of course, white women ourselves were an owned people, too. We had no rights of any kind. We must not confuse human rights with more comfortable status and consumer privileges.

Old records in surviving enslaver correspondence and diaries remind us that when individual settler men enjoyed a particular New Afrikan rape victim so much that they decided to move her into his house alongside his white woman and children, that this, too, was within his legitimate authority. One white mistress burst into tears over her husband's orders to have his latest rape victim added to the family dinner table. The white wife threatened to have the Black woman lashed. But hubby simply reminded his up-on-the-pedestal white wife that he could always have *her* taken out, stripped and whipped just like the other slaves. Patriarchy. All good, all the time.

Things like the "deference ritual" were important to re-en-slavement. For after the Civil War, poor Southern white women and children, who were often sharecroppers themselves, lived little better on a material level than the former Afrikan captives. Scandals, after all, were soon to sweep euro-settler society about the deadly exploitation of multitudes of "mill children" laboring from dawn to dusk in the textile mills and coal mines. Those were about poor *white* working-class children. Euro-settler women and children were property themselves, of course, regardless of class and the pretensions of superior race. Many, many thousands were killed during the frequent child-births creating the large family labor pool that even the poorest white would-be patriarch wanted.

Forced motherhood was and still is among the most dangerous occupations in the world, like coal mining or mercenary soldiering or prostitution. It took a hundred years after the Civil War for rape in marriage to even start to become a crime. When all those wedding vows spoke of women promising to "submit" to their husbands, they weren't talking about frying the eggs sunny-side up. To "submit" meant to submit physically. To make your body available for all the sex and child-bearing that the man of the house wanted. Those stranger-than-shit "born again" Christian marriage vows still like to keep that "submit" wording in the contract even today. Lots of men of all kinds today still think that this is their right—it is *their* world, isn't it?

In the South or North, being used as punching bags for male owners whether father or husband was so universal an experience for white women and children that it was not only legal but socially accepted as "natural." It is a shifty habit for patriarchal capitalism to always put the blame for their worst male crimes on "Mother Nature," like the Nazis tried to justify their Aryan nightmare. Settler women needed military capacity and strategy just to defend themselves, too. So patriarchal capitalism really had to have every little cup of racist addiction. To convince its white working-class women that they, too, should support the system as fellow "masters."

To Sum Things Up

During the Civil War and after 1865, New Afrikan women led a limited strategy of rebellion both spontaneous and conscious. Away from patriarchal capitalism and its attempts to re-enslave them. Living their communal culture created for survival during captivity. Mass withholding of their labor from plantations, insistence on their right to reject full-time wage labor, fighting to regain control over their bodies in production and reproduction both, New Afrikan women in particular cracked the old plantation system. For without the mass labor gangs the old plantation system couldn't work. The compromise they forced on the planter capitalists, even within the larger setback for liberation during the fall of Black Reconstruction, was the semi-feudal sharecropping system. Where families tilled fields and raised their children without white overseers although under the onerous class conditions of a defeated communal nation.

Cruel as the re-enslavement known as Segregation was, it did not exist completely unchecked. Author Zora Neal Hurston and SNCC Executive Secretary Ruby Doris Smith of the militant 1960s Sit-In movement in the South, were among the many New Afrikans to remind us that growing up in that post-Black Reconstruction South, they had been shielded as much as possible by their families and communities from the dehumanization of the colonial occupation. Growing up with love and confidence.

Although circumscribed, their childhood had been sustained by New Afrikan teachers and New Afrikan neighbors and clubs and sports teams in a sheltering framework. Before, living and working as captives in mass labor gangs under what were prison guards had produced one kind of violent childhood. After that, living in an oppressed New Afrikan society, with farms and social institutions that involuntarily served the occupying power but were operated by themselves, produced a different kind of childhood. Not that any of that still wasn't within what had been a crushing defeat for the older generations.

New Afrikan women no less than men fought to raise new generations of youth that had the self-confidence to succeed. The abilities to be players in the world. Were ready to be free. As Malcolm X often reminded his people in Harlem, Moses could liberate his people from captivity under Pharaoh but even Moses himself was not permitted by Jehovah to enter the Promised Land. The Jews of the old testament had to spend 40 years in the Wilderness before then. For no Jew born into slavery was fit to build the new free society. When i look at how distorted women who have grown up ruled by men are, myself included, i believe that we as well must go through the Wilderness.

New Afrikan women's strategy back then grew spontaneously out of their daily lives, their experiences and needs. Not out of some textbook or some political protest routine. Stubbornly living communal culture and fighting capitalism is often ignored or dismissed as "impractical." Yet and again, it was that partial strategy by women back then that proved most useful in real life. Still, it did not make that very difficult hurdle from the level of spontaneous breakout to the level of conscious strategy. In which analysis, tentative strategic understanding, new tactics & practice, criticism of results, and then the emergence of new strategy, all flow in a continuous dialectical circle of struggle. And those partial women's struggles & victories, great as they were, underline the reality that if you don't have a strategy to end a war then someone else will usually end it for you. But you won't like it.

All these earlier battles throughout the New Afrikan nation still throw light for us on the latest battlefield. And on battles certain to come.

(not the end)

Acknowledgement

i am not a herstorian, but use a lot of herstory in my work. While i've learned from more sisters than can easily point to here, there are some whose insightfulness shaped this essay. My thanks to them:

Paula Giddings ❖ *Jacqueline Jones* ❖ *Deborah Gray White*

Butch

Amazon Nation or Aryan Nation: White Women and the Coming of Black Genocide

Bottomfish Blues • 978-1-894946-55-1
168 pages • $12.95

The two main essays in this book come from the radical women's newspaper Bottomfish Blues, which was published in the late 1980s and early '90s; while a historical appendix on "The Ideas of Black Genocide in the Amerikkkan Mind" was written more recently, but only circulated privately. These texts provide raw and vital lessons at the violent crash scene of nation, gender, and class, from a revolutionary and non-academic perspective.

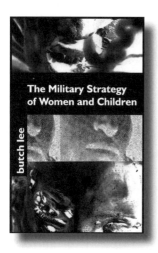

The Military Strategy of Women and Children

Butch Lee • 0973143231
116 pages • $12.00

Lays out the need for an autonomous and independent women's revolutionary movement, a revolutionary women's culture that involves not only separating oneself from patriarchal imperialism, but also confronting, opposing, and waging war against it by all means necessary.

Night-Vision: Illuminating War and Class on the Neo-Colonial Terrain

Butch Lee and Red Rover • 1883780004
187 pages • $14.95

bell hooks: "Night-Vision was so compelling to me because it has a spirit of militancy which reformist feminism tries to kill because militant feminism is seen as a threat to the liberal bourgeois feminism that just wants to be equal with men. It has that raw, unmediated truth-telling which I think we are going to need in order to deal with the fascism that's upon us."
A foundational analysis of post-modern capitalism, the decline of u.s. hegemony, and the need for a revolutionary movement of the oppressed to overthrow it all.

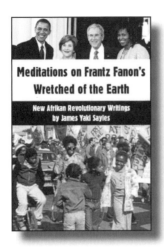

Meditations on Frantz Fanon's Wretched of the Earth: New Afrikan Revolutionary Writings

James Yaki Sayles • 978-1-894946-32-2
399 pages • $20.00

One of those who eagerly picked up Fanon in the '60s, who carried out armed expropriations and violence against white settlers, Sayles reveals how, behind the image of Fanon as race thinker, there is an underlying reality of antiracist communist thought. "This exercise is about more than our desire to read and understand Wretched (as if it were about some abstract world, and not our own); it's about more than our need to understand (the failures of) the anti-colonial struggles on the African continent. This exercise is also about us, and about some of the things that We need to understand and to change in ourselves and our world." —James Yaki Sayles

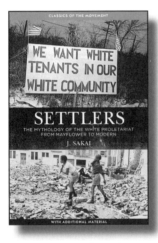

Settlers: The Mythology of the White Proletariat from Mayflower to Modern

J. Sakai • 978-1-62963-037-3
456 pages • $20.00

J. Sakai shows how the United States is a country built on the theft of Indigenous lands and Afrikan labor, on the robbery of the northern third of Mexico, the colonization of Puerto Rico, and the expropriation of the Asian working class, with each of these crimes being accompanied by violence. In fact, America's white citizenry have never supported themselves but have always resorted to exploitation and theft, culminating in acts of genocide to maintain their culture and way of life. This movement classic lays it all out, taking us through this painful but important history.

KER
SPL
EBE
DEB

Since 1998 Kersplebedeb has been an important source of radical literature and agit prop materials.

The project has a non-exclusive focus on anti-patriarchal and anti-imperialist politics, framed within an anticapitalist perspective. A special priority is given to writings regarding armed struggle in the metropole, and the continuing struggles of political prisoners and prisoners of war.

The Kersplebedeb website presents historical and contemporary writings by revolutionary thinkers from the anarchist and communist traditions.

Kersplebedeb can be contacted at:

Kersplebedeb
CP 63560
CCCP Van Horne
Montreal, Quebec
Canada
H3W 3H8

email: info@kersplebedeb.com
web: www.kersplebedeb.com
           www.leftwingbooks.net

Kersplebedeb